CW01665046

If you like this book, please consider leaving a review on Amazon. Leaving reviews helps me to grow the business and continue to create excellent resources for your children.

11+ Creative Writing Workbook.

About the author.

Philip O'Hanlon has been teaching English in one shape or another for over 25 years. Much of his experience has been in an international context having taught in both British and American schools. He studied Philosophy and English Literature at Manchester University before obtaining a PhD in Political Philosophy from Queen's University, Belfast. These days he privately coaches students towards gaining entry to their chosen schools and colleges and designs bespoke educational materials to assist this.

DR PHIL'S ENGLISH

Copyright © 2024 Dr Phil's English

11+ Creative Writing Workbook.

All rights reserved.

No part of this book may be reproduced or stored in a retrieval system, or transmitted in any form or by any means, electronic, mechanical, photocopying, recording, or otherwise, without express written permission of the author or publisher.

If you like this book you may also like 11+ Poetry Analysis Guide and 11+ Poetry Comprehension which can be purchased at Amazon.co.uk

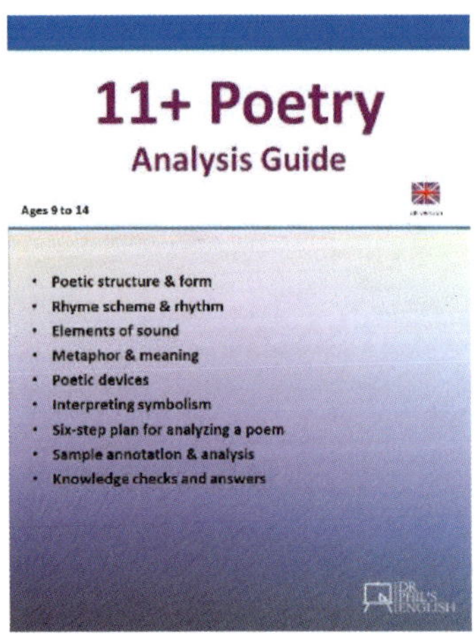

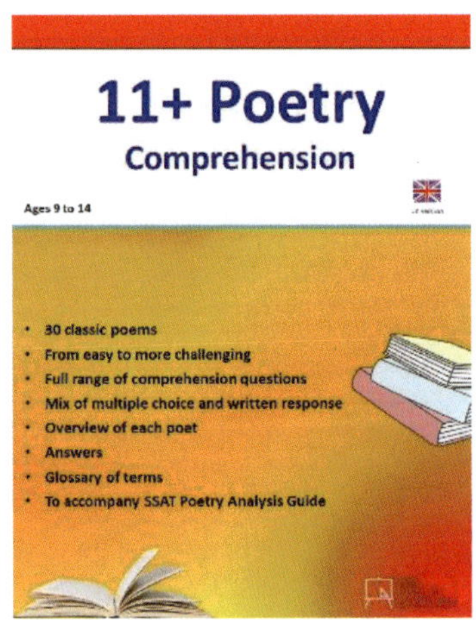

Table of Contents

Preface.

11+ tests (and other selective entry tests, as well as GCSE English) typically require candidates either to produce a piece of descriptive writing, based on a picture or prompt, or to write a narrative. While there is a lot of overlap, these two different types of writing require different approaches and techniques. Narrative writing should include lots of good descriptions, but it also needs plot, characters and action, which purely descriptive writing does not have. The present book covers both types of writing: it contains all the key elements that young learner needs to be able to master the 11+ creative writing component, including:

- basic elements of composition (sentence construction, parts of speech)
- clauses
- punctuation
- language devices (similes, metaphors, personification, etc.)
- 'show don't tell'
- imagery
- plot
- setting
- narrative tension
- characterisation and more.

There are also annotated exemplars, descriptive writing scaffolds, exam tips and plenty of exercises to allow learners to practise their skills. Answers are provided at the back of the book. Like my 11+ poetry books, it has been written principally with 11+ and 12+ students in mind, but the book is not limited to this cohort and will be useful to all children in the 9 – 14 age bracket who need to develop their creative writing skills. I hope you and your child / student enjoy the book and if you find it useful, please consider leaving a review on Amazon. This helps me to understand your requirements better and to continue to make the best resources targeted to your child's needs.

1. Introduction.

Welcome to the 11+ creative writing guide. In this book you will cover everything you need to become a skilled creative writer and to smash the 11+ creative writing test. First, let's go through some basics.

To improve your creative writing, you will need:

- A wide vocabulary
- Good spelling, punctuation and grammar
- Precise, detailed and vivid language (including verbs, nouns, adjectives and adverbs)
- Figurative language (metaphors, similes, personification, alliteration, onomatopoeia, etc.)
- A good imagination

We will cover all these things in this book and more.

As you go through the book there will be tonnes of exercises for you to practise your skills. You will find answers to all the tasks at the back of the book. Don't try to read too much at once. Take your time and work through the book thoroughly.

TEST TIP. Creative writing is not easy. Creative writing under test conditions is even harder. You have to come up with brilliant and dazzling descriptions in a very short time. To prepare for the exam, you need to start building up your store of descriptive phrases and story ideas that you can use whenever they are needed. Make sure you get a creative writing notebook to note down any **new vocabulary** and **descriptive phrases**. The more you prepare and memorise your descriptions and story ideas now, the easier the test will be. Practice makes perfect.

The importance of reading.

The best way to learn anything new is to follow a master or expert. With writing, it's no different. When we read good books, we are learning how to write from those who have already mastered the skill. That's why reading is one of the most important things you can do to improve your writing. The more you read, the better your writing will become.

Look at page 120 for a list of recommended books.

Be an active reader not a passive reader!

Being an **active** reader means paying **<u>very close attention</u>** to new vocabulary, unusual phrases, interesting descriptions, use of punctuation, and sentence structure. Be aware of how the writer is writing and think about why the writer might have chosen the particular words, phrases and sentence structures that they have. If you do this, you will boost your own writing skills much more quickly than if you read passively.

Passive reading is reading for pleasure.

Active reading is reading for <u>purpose</u>.

2. What is descriptive writing?

TASK 1.

Imagine for a moment that you visit a wonderful desert island. The island is the most beautiful and peaceful place you have ever seen, full of all the things a perfect paradise should have. Pause for a moment and consider all the things you might be able to see, hear, smell and feel on the desert island. Make a list of them in the boxes:

Things I can see.

Things I can hear.

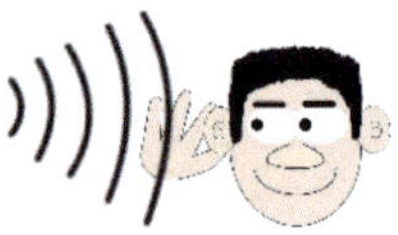

Things I can smell.

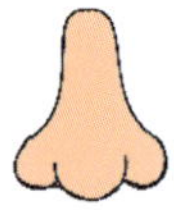

Things I can feel.

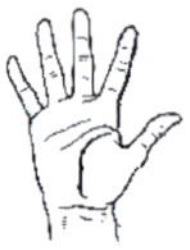

How many things did you think of? Look at page 122 for some suggestions.

Brainstorming ideas is an extremely important part of descriptive writing. You should be able to generate as many ideas as possible before beginning to write. Don't worry if you weren't able to think of so many ideas. By the end of this book, you should be able to think of a lot more.

What is descriptive writing?

Descriptive writing is all about creating images and experiences with words. Through your descriptive writing, you are aiming to create a world that your reader can *visualise* and experience as if they were ***actually there*** in that world. For example, when we describe a beautiful mountain scene, we want the reader to forget where they are for a moment and transport them to this world of beautiful mountains in all its rich detail. This is what we mean when we say we want the mountains to come alive for the reader. To do this well, it takes practice.

What descriptive writing is not.

Descriptive writing is **NOT** narrative writing. Narrative writing is story writing and includes a plot, a beginning, middle and end, characters, and action. Narrative writing includes descriptive writing, but descriptive writing should not include narrative. If you have been asked to write a story, then write a story, using good descriptions. But if you have only been asked to write a description, do not write a story. Many learners fall into this trap when responding to descriptive writing questions. They run out of things to say and their descriptions slowly turn into narratives.

TASK 2.

Look at the two examples below, see if you can identify which is a narrative and which is a description. If you are unsure, look at page 122 for the answer.

The Ascent.

Samantha stared at the towering rock face, a mixture of excitement and nervousness coursing through her veins. The annual rock-climbing competition was just a week away, and she had been training relentlessly for this moment. Her climbing partner, Jake, stood beside her, a reassuring smile on his face.

"Are you ready for this, Sam?" Jake asked, adjusting his harness.

Samantha nodded, her heart pounding. "I've been preparing for months. We've got this."

They had chosen a challenging route that required precision and strength. As they began their ascent, Samantha felt the cool breeze on her face, the sun casting long shadows on the rocks. She could hear the cheers of fellow climbers below, urging them on.

Halfway up, they encountered a particularly tricky section, a narrow ledge with minimal handholds. Samantha's fingers ached as she reached for the next grip. "This is tough," she admitted, her voice trembling.

Jake glanced at her, his eyes filled with determination. "We can't give up now, Sam. Remember why we're doing this."

Samantha thought of their friend, Lily, who was battling cancer. The climbing competition was a fundraiser to help cover Lily's medical expenses. With renewed determination, Samantha and Jake pushed forward, each move calculated and deliberate. Finally, they reached the top, the sense of accomplishment washing over them. They had conquered the challenge, not just for themselves but for Lily and all those fighting their own battles.

As they descended, Samantha couldn't help but reflect on the power of determination and the support of a true friend. The competition was just the beginning of their journey, but they knew that together, they could face any challenge that came their way.

The Mountainside.

The morning sun ascended over the horizon, casting its golden rays across the rugged landscape. Towering beasts of stone, the mountains, stood solemnly, their peaks veiled in mist, as if shrouded in ancient secrets. The river, a meandering ribbon of crystal blue, wound its way through the valley, splashing and lapping in a rhythm that harmonised with the rustling leaves.

A meadow at the base of the mountains burst into a garden of wildflowers, painting the earth with vibrant hues. Delicate blossoms nodded in the gentle breeze, as if exchanging secrets with the sunlight that filtered through the pine trees above. Oaks and maples, their branches outstretched in an emerald embrace, whispered tales of centuries gone by.

In the distance, an old barn stood strong and proud – its timbers bearing the scars of time. Moss crept up its sides, adding a touch of lime to its weathered face. It had ivory walls and a solid oak door. The slate tiles on the roof were shimmering in the sunlight while the windows seemed as though they had not been cleaned for years. Snaking out of the chimney, a thin plume of smoke drifted off into the heavens.

Amongst the trees, squirrels darted and chattered while sparrows and swallows sang cheerful tunes that echoed through the valley. A family of deer, graceful as dancers, moved through the forest with a quiet elegance.

Above, the sky stretched out like a cyan blanket with cotton-white clouds that drifted lazily on a gentle breeze. The mountains seemed to touch the sky, their peaks veiled in wisps of cloud. It was a scene of spectacular beauty, where time seemed to stand still.

3. Basic elements of English composition.

The building blocks of good descriptive writing are **verbs**, **nouns**, **adjectives** and **adverbs**. In this section we will work on improving your skills in using these different parts of speech, so your writing is as strong as it can be.

Task 3.

Identify the nouns, verbs, adjectives and adverbs. Sort them into correct boxes below. Answers are at the back of the book.

elegance ginormous tree observe sometimes lighthouse meadow cautiously majestic compose practice chuckle pain well incredible speedily fast float never gallery persuade saunter ocean practise elegant incredibly calm suddenly graceful peculiar amble gallop wither sunset chess complicated jubilant intensely often meticulously

Nouns	Verbs

Adjectives	Adverbs

Verbs.

What is a verb? A verb is usually an action word (or "doing" word). For example, verbs such as "walk", "talk", "drive" or "shout" express an action. Most verbs are actions words like this, but not all are. There are some verbs which express a ***state of being*** rather than an action. These types of verbs are indicated with the "be" verb. For example, "I am Philip" and "he is tall" express states of being using different forms of the "be" verb ("am" and "is").

Types of Verbs

Doing Verbs | **Being Verbs**

Something I do | **Something I am**

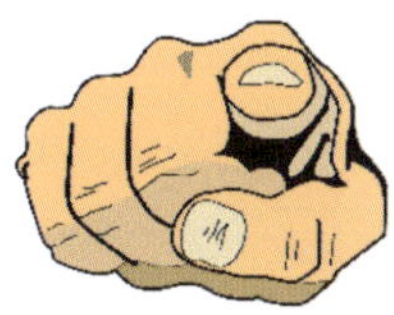

You study

You are students

Descriptive verbs for *walk*

Amble	Hike	Nudge	Rocket	Step	Tread	Voyage
Bumble	Leap	Parade	Rove	Dart	Trek	Worm
Cruise	Limp	Plod	Saunter	Stride	Trot	Wander
Dawdle	Lope	Prowl	Scurry	Stroll	Trudge	Weave
Gallop	March	Ramble	Shuffle	Tiptoe	Veer	Wiggle
Glide	Meander	Roam	Skip	Traipse	Venture	Zigzag

tip: Verbs are the most important element for descriptive writing. Verbs carry the action and energy of the scene you are describing.

Always aim to use lots of verbs, making them as precise and as interesting as you can.

Key point: **Avoid boring, non-descriptive verbs. Replace them with stronger, more interesting, more descriptive verbs.**

TASK 4.

Underline all the verbs in the Passage to the right.

It was 5pm. The rain was heavy. It fell continuously, while Jack walked home from work. As soon as he arrived home, he opened the door and went inside. He took off his coat, sat down in the chair and slept.

Now look at the version below which uses stronger and more descriptive verbs.

It was 5pm. The rain hammered down. It splashed and splattered continuously, while Jack trudged home from work. Upon arrival, Jack flung the door open and shot inside. He threw off his coat, slumped into the chair and drifted off into a dream world.

TASK 5.

Rewrite the passage below using more descriptive verbs.

It was 5pm. The sun shone down on the valley. Its rays of heat shone on Jack's face. The gentle breeze blew through the trees. The trees moved from side to side. High above, clouds moved across the sky. Birds flew high into the clouds. Mountains were surrounding the town. In the garden, children were eating ice cream and dogs were jumping in the air.

Precise verbs: more examples.

The man walked along the path.	**The man <u>strolled</u> along the path.**
The boulder fell to earth.	**The boulder <u>plummeted</u> to earth.**
Water hit against the rocks.	**Water <u>crashed</u> against the rocks.**
The wind blew noisily.	**The wind <u>howled</u>.**

TASK 6.

Find more descriptive verbs to replace the boring verbs.

The dog walked along the street.

____

The train moved quickly down the track.

____

The girl drank her cola quickly.

____

The mouse ate the cheese.

____

The cow chewed the grass.

____

I love chocolate ice cream.

____

Jenny walked in the park.

____

Rain hit against the roof.

____

The wind blew against the trees.

____

Leaves moved in the breeze.

____

Nouns.

What is a noun? A noun is a word that names something, such as a person, place, thing, or idea. For example, "book", "students", "London", "love" are all nouns. Most standard English sentences need at least one noun. However, nouns come in many forms and not all nouns are equally effective.

Key point: Avoid boring, non-descriptive nouns. Replace them with stronger, more interesting, more descriptive nouns.

Look at these examples:

"The dog sauntered into the room."

Although the **verb** is effective, the sentence doesn't tell us much about the dog or the room. But if we replace "dog" with "pug" and "room" with "kitchen" then readers will get a more vivid image in their mind. Here are some more examples:

The house was surrounded by lots of trees.	→	**The bungalow was surrounded by lots of oak and pine.**
A person was driving his car dangerously down the road.	→	**The elderly man was speeding down the lane in his Ferrari.**
Sam ate his food quickly.	→	**Sam shovelled his fish and chips down his throat.**
Graceful birds circled above.	→	**Graceful swallows and sparrows circled above.**

Precise nouns allow you to do two things:

- **add more detail and descriptiveness**
- **become more concise**

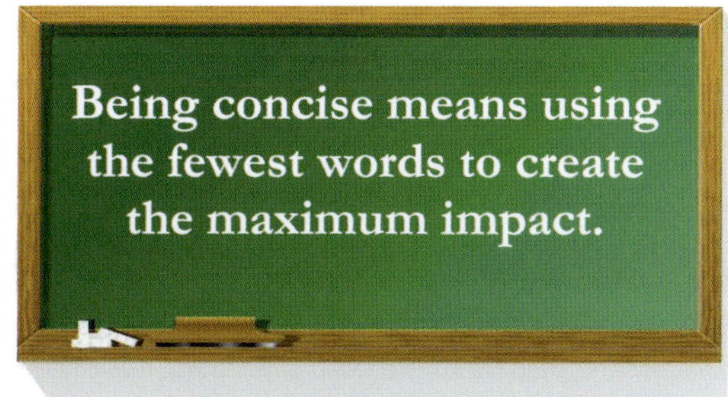

TASK 7.

Read the passage below. First, identify the nouns and then replace the boring nouns with more descriptive nouns. You may also use adjectives if you wish.

Tom unhooked the latch on the door and went into the garden. He saw beautiful flowers and some water. Birds circled above and a dog lay in the grass. There were people sitting on a piece of material, eating food. Tall trees cast long shadows across the street. There was a path that ran through the garden. He followed the path and came to a building. Outside the building there was a parked car and two people playing a game. Another person was riding an animal.

Now re-write the passage using more descriptive nouns.

TASK 8.

Re-write the sentences below using more descriptive or more concise nouns.

1. The person was playing an instrument.

____

2. My child likes to play sport. ______________________________

3. There was an insect crawling across the furniture.

____

4. The liquid began to burn.

____

5. We travelled across the ocean in a kind of boat that hovers over the water.

____

6. The leader of the country stepped inside a long vehicle and departed.

____

7. Mike turned the corner and saw a large building.

____

8. In the army soldiers use clothing that allows them to blend into their surroundings.

____

9. The garden was full of trees.

____

Adjectives.

Adjectives are words that describe or modify nouns or pronouns, providing additional information about their qualities, characteristics, or features. They add details and enhance the meaning of a sentence by answering questions like "what kind?" or "how many?" Adjectives can express various qualities such as size, colour, shape, appearance, emotions, opinions, and more. For example, "The tiny ant", "an icy morning", "her immaculate house", "his angry manner" all include adjectives.

Use strong and interesting adjectives to improve your Descriptions, but DO NOT overuse them. Adjectives (like most linguistic techniques) are like seasoning for food: if you add a bit of salt and pepper to your food it will enhance the taste, but too much can destroy it!

Look at the examples below:

- ✗ The mountain appeared to be awakening from its slumber. (No adjective)
- ✗ The **big** mountain appeared to be awakening from its slumber. (Bland adjective)
- ✗ The **huge**, **amazing**, **spectacular grey** mountain…. (Too many adjectives)
- ✓ The **gigantic, silver** mountain appeared to be awakening.... (Just right)
- ✗ The old castle, which was in a poor condition, stood proudly. (bland adjectives)
- ✓ The **ancient**, **dilapidated** castle stood proudly. (Just right)

Look at the sentences below and identify which sentence has no adjectives, which uses bland adjectives, which uses too many adjectives, and which is just right.

1. The blue sky reflected in the blue lake.
2. The sky reflected in the lake.
3. The azure sky reflected in the silky, sapphire lake.
4. The amazing, deep blue sky reflected in the sparkling, majestic grey-blue lake.

Sometimes it's better to replace an adjective with a verb. Look below:

With bland adjectives: "The old building was really big."

With stronger adjectives: "The ancient building was gigantic."

With adjective + verb: "The ageing castle **towered** over the valley."

This last sentence **shows** rather than **tells** us that the building was big without using an adjective; it replaces a bland adjective with a more precise and impactful verb.

TASK 9.

Read the passage below and replace any boring nouns and adjective with more descriptive ones.

It was a nice day. The yellow sun was shining and the blue sky was amazing. The house was big. It had a red wooden door and a metal frame. It had a nice garden with nice flowers. Big green trees stretched upwards to touch the lovely white clouds. Within its walls, a beautiful living room featured a beautiful wooden bookshelf. The family enjoyed a good dinner at the nice dining table, surrounded by warmth and love.

Colours.

Colours are adjectives (as well as nouns) and they offer a fantastic opportunity to add extra detail and descriptiveness to your writing. However, the same rule applies to colours as applies to regular adjectives: do not choose bland or boring colours for your descriptions, such as "blue" or "red"; choose unusual and interesting ones. See the options you have below.

Blue
Cyan
Sapphire
Azure
Midnight-blue

Red
Scarlet
Crimson
Ruby
Blood-red

Green
Emerald
Forest-green
Lime
Pine-green

White
Snow-white
Ivory
Apple-white
Pure white

Black
Jet-black
Ink-black
Coal-black
Charcoal

Grey
Dolphin-grey
Slate-grey
Silver
Ash

Yellow
Mustard
Lemon
Golden
Amber

Brown
Mud-brown
Auburn
Beige
Chocolate

Purple
Violet
Plum
Indigo
Lilac

Example sentences:

The **scarlet** sunset painted the evening sky, casting a mesmerising glow over the horizon.

The **azure** ocean stretched endlessly before us.

Amidst the lush **emerald** forest, a glistening lake sparkled under the sunlight.

As night descended, the **indigo** sky emerged, adorned with a blanket of twinkling stars.

Task 10.

Write 8 descriptive sentences using unusual colours.

1. (sky) ____________________

____

2. (ocean) ____________________

____

3. (hair) ____________________

____

4. (sunshine) ____________________

____

5. (forest) ____________________

____

6. ____________________

____

7. ____________________

____

8. ____________________

____

Adverbs.

Adverbs are used to modify verbs (and sometimes adjectives). Many of them can be recognised easily by their ending in -ly (like 'easily'). However, not all adverbs end in -ly. For example, adverbs of time or place rarely end in -ly.

Adverbs of time:

Now, later, earlier, yesterday, tomorrow, tonight, soon, yet, today.

Adverbs of place:

Here, there, everywhere, nowhere, somewhere, anywhere, in, out, inside, outside, wherever, on, off, over, under, away, left, right, north, south, east, west. (Some of these can also be prepositions, depending on their place and function in the sentence).

> **Warning**: adverbs slow the pace of your writing, which may or may not be a good thing, depending on what you are trying to do. But they can also make your descriptions seem wordy and clunky. Many adverbs do not add much to the meaning of the sentence and are often (but not always) a bad replacement for effective verbs. Before using an adverb, consider the rules below:

Adverb rules.

- **Rule 1.** Consider whether the adverb is needed or whether it adds anything to the meaning of your description. If not, delete it.

- **Rule 2.** If you decide an adverb is needed, make sure to **avoid** weak, bland adverbs in favour of strong and interesting ones.

Bland adverbs include words such as 'really', 'very', 'extremely' etc., as these adverbs do not add meaning or value to your sentence. In most cases such adverbs can either be left out or replaced with a more effective verb. Consider the following on the next page:

Verb + bland adverb:

"The car moved **really quickly** along the track." (verb + adverb). ✗

Strong verb without adverb.

"The car sped / rocketed / zoomed along the track." (strong verb and no adverb). ✓

More examples:

"The wind **whispered quietly** across the valley." (Redundant adverb). ✗

The adverb 'quietly' here is redundant (meaning useless); its meaning is already contained in the meaning of the word 'whisper' and so it adds nothing to the sentence. Delete it!

"The girl **screamed loudly**." (Redundant adverb). ✗

Again, screaming is already loud and so the adverb adds no further meaning to the sentence. Delete it!

"The river **moved slowly** through the valley." ✗

"The river **meandered**." ✓

Quick knowledge check.

What is a redundant adverb? ______________________________

Give an example of a bland adverb? ______________________

Give an example of a weak verb: ________________________

Give an example of a strong verb: _______________________

What is another colour-word you can use for red? _________________

What is another colour-word for blue? ______________________

TASK 11.

Read the following descriptive passage. Highlight all the adjectives and adverbs.

It was 12am midnight. Kingsley was on his final mission. The cold, icy air penetrated his skin sharply. The bright moon, which was shining intensely through the clouds, hung in the sky like a precious, pure pearl; its glowing light spread thoroughly across the dark blue sky. Kingsley looked straight ahead and could just about see a dark silhouette forming vaguely on the horizon. As he moved steadily closer, the vague silhouette turned gradually into the definite, clear contours of a house standing eerily over the valley. At either side of the house there were different types of extremely tall, green trees, standing proudly and protectively like night watchmen. The house seemed to be watching him intently. Up above, a black raven hovered suspiciously over the house. The total, sinister silence was brazenly broken only by the distant, faraway sounds of wolves howling menacingly. Kingsley, who was now feeling really scared, walked forward cautiously.

TASK 12.

Re-write and improve.

Re-write the above passage.

1. Remove any redundant adverbs or adjectives (or any other redundant words).
2. Replace any weak adjectives or adverbs with stronger ones.
3. If you can replace adverbs or adjectives with strong verbs, do that.
4. Aim to make the writing more concise (less wordy).

____

____

____

____

4. Simple, compound & complex sentences.

Examiners need to see a <u>varied use of sentence forms</u>. At a minimum, this includes using, simple, compound and complex sentences. We will take a look at that soon, but before looking in more detail at these types of sentences, we need to look at <u>**clauses**</u>.

What is a clause?

A clause is a part of a sentence that contains two things:

i) a subject

ii) a predicate

The subject is the thing or person that the sentence is about; it is usually represented by a noun or noun phrase such as "I" or "The book", and typically comes before a verb. The predicate is everything after the subject that tells us something about the subject.

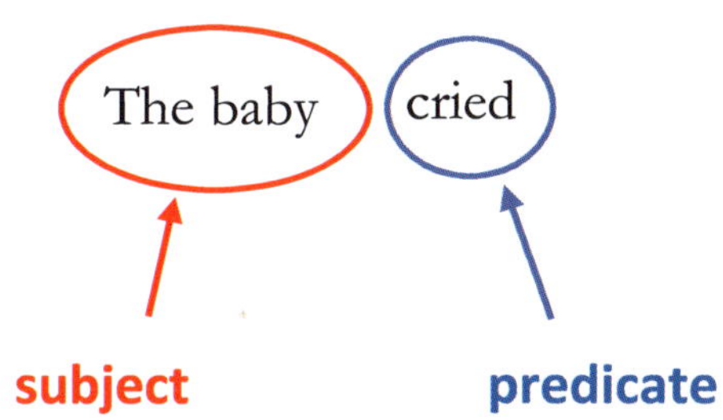

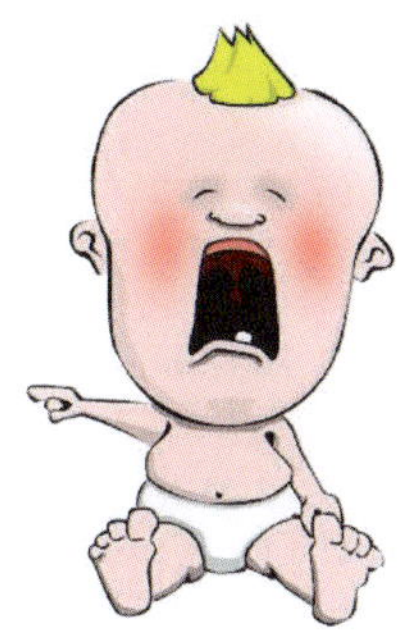

Sometimes, the predicate is simply the verb part of a clause or sentence. However, the predicate can include direct objects too.

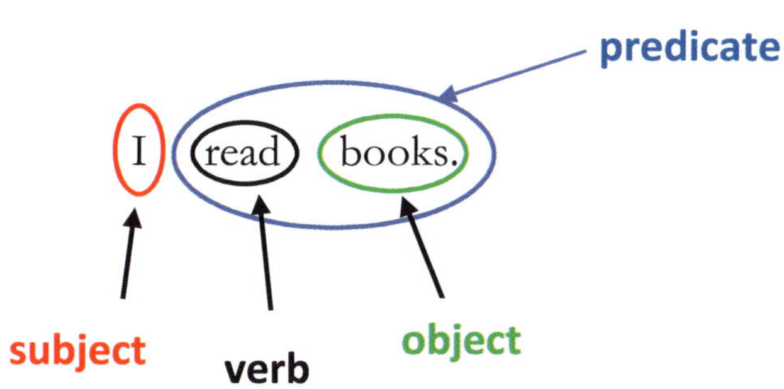

Quick check. True or false:

The subject comes before the predicate. __________

The subject modifies the noun. __________

The predicate tells us something about the noun. __________

The subject is the thing that the sentence is about. __________

Independent and dependent clauses.

There are two types of clause that you need to know: <u>independent</u> and <u>dependent</u> clauses (sometimes called main and subordinate clauses).

What on earth is an independent clause?

An independent clause is a clause that contains a subject and predicate, and <u>**which makes sense on its own**</u>. In other words, an independent clause is a clause which expresses a <u>complete idea</u> and does not need anything else to complete it. For this reason, independent clauses can also be complete sentences on their own.

For example, "I like pizza" is an independent clause because it expresses a complete idea and makes sense on its own. We could place a full-stop after it and that would make it a complete sentence.

What on earth is a dependent clause?

A dependent clause <u>**does not make sense on its own**</u> and does not express a complete idea. For that reason, it cannot form a complete sentence on its own. This is why we call a dependent clause *dependent*, because it is dependent on something else (an independent clause) to complete it. For example, "Although I generally like pizza" is not a complete idea. "Although" is what we call a <u>subordinating conjunction</u>, and it indicates that we are dealing with a dependent clause – a clause that needs another clause to complete it. The full sentence should be "Although I generally like pizza, I don't like pineapple pizza."

Types of clause

Independent clause (main clause)

Contains a subject & a verb.
Makes sense on its own.
Can form a complete sentence.

Dependent clause (subordinate clause)

Contains a subject & a verb.
Does <u>not</u> express a complete thought.
<u>Cannot</u> form its own sentence.

Coordinating conjunctions

For, and, nor, but, or, yet, so
(FANBOYS)

Subordinating conjunctions

Although, after, because, before, if, since, unless, until, when, whenever, where, whereas, while, whether, as, as long as, etc.

Example sentences.

<u>Dependent clauses are underlined.</u>
Independent clauses are not underlined.

I need to finish my homework.

<u>Because she loves to read books</u>, she often visits the library.

<u>After they went to the park yesterday</u>, they had a picnic.

He enjoys playing the guitar.

We decided to go for a walk <u>since the sun was shining brightly</u>.

<u>Although he enjoys playing the guitar</u>, he rarely performs in public.

They went to the park yesterday.

I went to the store <u>before going to the party</u>.

TASK 13.

Place a "D" next to the sentence if it includes a dependent clause. Place an "I" next to the sentence if it only contains an independent clause or clauses. Underline any dependent clauses. The first one is done for you.

1. <u>When I need to finish my homework</u>, I stay up late. __D_
2. I don't like sprouts. _____
3. Before I go out, I must take a shower. _____
4. I want to travel the world and taste different types of cuisine. _____
5. I will deal with that problem after I return from work. _____
6. The Nile is the longest river in the world. _____
7. It rains a lot in London though it doesn't snow too often. _____
8. It rained last night, but it wasn't very heavy. _____
9. Too many cooks spoil the broth. _____
10. Never let a fool kiss you, or a kiss fool you. _____
11. I'll join you as long as you don't stay too late. _____
12. Although I'm not the biggest fan of Star Wars, I went to see it anyway. _____
13. If I win the lottery, I'll share half with you. _____
14. The best things in life are free. _____
15. The best things in life are free, and I like free stuff. _____

Now that you understand the difference between independent and dependent clauses, we can move on to simple, compound and complex sentences.

A **simple sentence** – a sentence that contains one independent clause.

Example: "I like pizza."

A **compound sentence** – a sentence which we form by combining two independent clauses. We can combine two independent clauses either with a co-ordinating conjunction (and, or, but etc.,) or with a semi-colon.

Making a compound sentence with a co-ordinating conjunction:

You may have heard of **FANBOYS** before. If you haven't, it stands for For, And, Not, But, Or, Yet, and So. These are the **coordinating conjunctions** you can use to combine two independent clauses together into a compound sentence.

For example:

"I like pizza. I don't like chips." becomes "I like pizza, **but** I don't like chips".

Other examples:

"I like pizza, **so** I will have one more piece."
"I like pizza, **and** I am going to order one now."

NOTE: We often place a comma before the conjunction in longer compound sentences.
"I like playing football with friends, **and** I like playing chess with my brother."

Making a compound sentence with semi-colons.

The other way to combine independent clauses to make a compound sentence is with a semi-colon. For example,

"I like oranges; I like apples."

"Jack drives a Porsche; Jenny drives a Ferrari."

"I don't have school on Friday; I think I will go to the park."

We have now covered simple and complex sentences; let's move onto complex sentences.

Complex sentences.

Complex sentences combine independent *and* dependent clauses. Below are some examples of complex sentences. Can you spot the dependent and independent clauses?

After I finish work, I will post your letter.

I don't like watching football although I do like playing it.

As Jimmy rode his bike, he encountered a bear.

As long as you don't disturb me, I'll stay here.

I won't be going to the cinema unless you come with me.

Were you able to identify the dependent and independent clauses? The dependent clause is highlighted in yellow while the independent clause is unhighlighted. You can see that the dependent clause can be placed either before the independent clause or after it; the order doesn't usually matter. However, you might also have spotted that when the dependent clause is first, it is usually followed by a comma, whereas the comma is not required when the dependent clause comes after the independent clause.

Key point: To score high marks in your writing make sure you use a variety of sentence forms, including simple, compound & complex sentences.

TASK 14.

Identify whether you think the sentence is simple, compound or complex.

1. She walked to the park. _______________

2. While she was walking to the park, she spotted a colourful butterfly. _______________

3. The beautiful sun was shining brightly. _______________

4. Although the sun was shining brightly, it felt chilly in the breeze. _______________

5. He decided to go for a swim, but he realised he forgot his swimsuit. _______________

6. The cat meowed loudly. _______________

7. When the cat meowed loudly, it was asking for attention. _______________

8. They baked cookies for the school fundraiser. _______________

9. They baked cookies for school, and they sold them all in a few hours. _______________

10. She walked to the park, and her friends joined her. _______________

11. The sun was rising but it was still cold. _______________

12. I like going to Spain because it's warm there. _______________

13. The quick, brown fox jumped over the lazy cat. _______________

14. What is it like to grow up on a farm? _______________

15. I won't go out unless it stops raining. _______________

5. Punctuation.

Punctuation is important. We need it to organise and structure our writing effectively, to create emphasis and to make our meanings clear. There's no need to fear punctuation. It's not difficult to learn some simple rules of effective punctuation, and once you have mastered them you will be set for life. Here we provide just an outline of some of the most important punctuation rules.

> **Key point: To score high marks in your creative writing make sure to use a variety of punctuation – not just commas and full stops. This may include semi-colons, colons, dash, exclamation mark and other items.**

In this section we are going to look at the following:

Comma	**,**
Semi-colon	**;**
Colon	**:**
Apostrophe	**'**
Exclamation mark	**!**
Ellipse	**…**
Hyphens	**-**
Dash	**–**

"Let's eat grandma!"

"Let's eat, grandma!"

Commas.

Along with full-stops, commas are probably the kind of punctuation you will use the most. Here is a list of 7 common uses.

1. To separate items in a list:

She bought apples, oranges, and bananas.

I play football, rugby, and tennis.

2. After an adverbial phrase at the start of the sentence:

In the evening, I went to the gym.

Suddenly, the room exploded.

3. To separate clauses in a compound sentence:

I don't like to play sport, but I like watching it.

4. To set apart additional, non-essential information from the rest of the sentence:

The cat, which is black, is sitting on your car.

The boy, who is 15, is incredibly annoying.

5. To separate direct quotations from the rest of the sentence:

John said, "I like pizza."
"I run every morning because it's good for my health," she said.

6. To separate contrasting elements:

His car was a BMW, not a Mercedes.

7. To separate coordinate adjectives:

The fluffy, silverish clouds inched across the sky.

Not using commas correctly can cause problems with communication. For example, compare these two sentences:

Sentence 1: **"Let's eat, Grandma!"** Sentence 2: **"Let's eat Grandma!"**

Can you see the difference in meaning? The comma in the first sentence shows that the speaker is talking to Grandma. The speaker is suggesting to Grandma that they eat. The second sentence has a very different meaning: it reads as a suggestion to eat the grandma! The presence of the comma completely changes the meaning. Look at another example:

"I want to thank my parents, Sara, and God."

"I want to thank my parents, Sara and God."

Can you see the difference in meaning this time? The first one is thanking multiple people (the parents and Sara) as well as thanking God. However, the second sentence makes it seem as though Sara and God are the names of the parents! Look at one more:

"The criminal said the judge is mad."

"The criminal, said the judge, is mad."

See the difference? The first tells us that the criminal said that the judge was mad, whereas in the second, the judge is telling us that the criminal was mad – very different meanings! Let's try one more:

"At the front of the garden gates have been fitted to stop the dog from escaping."

"At the front of the garden, gates have been fitted to stop the dog from escaping."

In this case, if we do not include a comma after "garden", the sentence does not make sense. If we include the comma, we understand that gates have been fitted at the front of the garden. So hopefully, with these simple examples, you should be able to see how important little old commas can be for effective communication.

TASK 15.

Are these sentences correct? If not, write the correct version below.

1. Jenny went to the store to buy milk cheese, chicken beans and meat.

2. Frequently my mom cleans my bedroom.

3. I can't stand the smell of fish but, I love the smell of lemon.

4. Jimmy's car which he bought, last year is in need of repair.

5. My favourite colour, is black not white.

6. My sister loves to play soccer, but she hates, basketball.

7. The small fluffy adorable puppy played in the sunny garden.

8. "I need help" she screamed.

9. While I was walking the dog, was barking.

10. All of a sudden Jim, jumped out of the water.

Semi-colons.

Semi-colons are a little trickier than commas. Most people are never sure how to use them. I am going to show you one simple way to use them so you can pick up extra points for punctuation in descriptive writing.

What is a semi-colon?

A semi-colon (;) is a punctuation mark used in writing to separate two closely related but independent clauses in a sentence. It is a combination between a comma and a full stop (stronger than a comma, but weaker than a full stop). The main purpose of a semi-colon is to show that the two clauses it separates are closely connected in meaning but that they could also stand alone as individual sentences if desired.

Here's an example of how to use a semi-colon:

1. "I have a meeting in the morning; I need to prepare my presentation."

In this sentence, the two clauses on either side of the semi-colon could be independent sentences by themselves. E.g.,

2. I have a meeting. I need to prepare my presentation.

However, the writer has chosen to link them together with a semi-colon to emphasise the close connection between having a meeting (clause 1) and the need to prepare a presentation (clause 2).

Make sure the clauses either side of the semi-colon are ***both*** independent ***and*** related.

related

The sun was setting on the horizon. It made the sky pink.

independent independent

The sun was setting on the horizon; it made the sky pink. ✓

NOT related

The sun was setting on the horizon. The dog barked.

independent | **independent**

The sun was setting on the horizon; the dog barked. ✗

The sun was setting on the horizon. The dog barked. ✓

related

Because the sun was setting on the horizon, the sky was pink.

NOT independent | **independent**

Because the sun was setting on the horizon; the sky was pink. ✗

Because the sun was setting on the horizon, the sky was pink. ✓

If unsure, the easiest way to use a semi-colon is to search through your writing for full stops. Then replace one of the full-stops with a semi-colon. But before you do that, make sure the two sentences either side of the full stop are closely related. "The sun was setting on the horizon. It made the sky pink" are related, and so can be separated with a semi-colon. The sentences "The sun was setting on the horizon. The dog barked" are not related, so it would be better to keep them separated by a full stop.

TASK 16.

Are the following sentences correct? If not, write the correct version below.

1. Because of the heavy snow this evening; we won't be going to work tomorrow.

____

2. The performance was great, tomorrow we will do it again.

____

3. I didn't go to the movies last night; although I wanted to.

____

4. The show was postponed; due to the lead actor getting sick.

____

5. As long as you promise not to tell anybody, I will tell you.

____

6. Waiting for the class to end, is boring.

____

7. I like playing basketball, but I'm not very good at it.

____

8. I like playing basketball; but I'm not very good at it.

____

9. The company launched a new product; it quickly gained popularity in the market.

____

10. The company launched a new product and, it quickly gained popularity in the market.

____

Colons.

In grammar, a colon (:) is a punctuation mark that is used to introduce or emphasise information in a sentence. It serves several purposes:

Introducing lists: A colon can be used to introduce a list of items or elements.

Example: "She bought some fruits from the store: apples, bananas, and oranges."
Example: "The meadow was full of glorious flowers: lilies, tulips, daisies and daffodils.

Introducing explanations.

Example: "The situation was clear: they had to act quickly."
Example: "The man's face was heavily burnt: he had been sitting in the sun all day."

Introducing quotations or speeches.

Example: "He started his speech with these words: 'Ladies and gentlemen, thank you for being here.'"

NOTE: the part before the colon should be an independent clause that can stand alone as a complete sentence. The information after the colon is usually related to, or explains, the information before the colon. There should be no space before the colon but a single space after it. Proper usage of colons can enhance clarity and add emphasis to your writing.

More examples:

- The forest at dusk was a sight to behold: tall, ancient trees stood proud, their branches reaching for the stars.
- It was a beautiful scene: a colourful sunset cast a warm, orange glow over the water, and silhouetted birds soared in the distance.
- The cityscape from the rooftop was breathtaking: skyscrapers pierced the sky, their illuminated windows forming a dazzling mosaic of urban life.

TASK 17.

Are the following sentences correct? If not, write the correct version below.

1. These animals are all amphibians: frogs, salamanders, newts and toads.

____

2. There is only one answer to the: problem sell your house.

____

3. I love France it's beautiful; and it has delicious food.

____

4. At the break of dawn, the majestic mountain range revealed itself in all its splendor snow-capped peaks glimmering in the golden hues of the rising sun.

____

5. The winners of this week's school quiz: are Jane, Imran and Felix.

____

6. Anderson Wang didn't know whether to order: pizza, pasta or fried rice.

____

7. She got what she deserved a new car and a fancy house.

____

8. Kingsley needs to: improve his use of the present perfect.

____

9. There were stone pillars standing in the field: the ruins of an ancient castle.

____

Apostrophes.

An apostrophe (') is a punctuation mark used for various things, but mostly to indicate possession and contraction.

Possession: When used to show possession, the apostrophe is usually placed before the "s" to indicate that something belongs to someone or something.

Example: "The dog's bone" (The bone belongs to the dog).

Example: "The tree's leaves" (The leaves belong to the tree).

However, when the noun already ends in "s" you can place the apostrophe after the "s" or add another "s" and put the apostrophe before it.

Example: "James' bike." Or "James's bike".

With a plural possessive noun that ends in "s", place the apostrophe after the "s".

Example: "My parents' house".

Possessive pronouns: "Its" (belonging to it), "yours" (belonging to you), "hers" (belonging to her), "theirs" (belonging to them).

NOTE: A common mistake is to use an apostrophe with the possessive pronoun "its" (e.g., "it's bone"). The possessive pronoun "its" is often confused with "it's" ("it is").

This is a mistake!

"The cat licked **its** paws and **it's** now grooming itself." ✓

In this sentence, *its* is used to show possession, indicating that the paws belong to the cat. On the other hand, *it's* is a contraction of "it is," used to describe the cat's current activity of grooming itself. **DO NOT** use an apostrophe with possessive pronouns.

<u>Contraction</u>: Apostrophes are used in contractions to combine two words into one by omitting one or more letter/s. Examples include:

"I can't" (short for "I cannot").

"it's" (short for "it is" or "it has").

"You're" (short for "You are").

"He'll" (short for "He will").

<u>NOTE</u>: apostrophes are **<u>not</u>** used to form plurals. For example, "apple's" is incorrect when referring to more than one apple. The correct form is "apples" without an apostrophe. This is a very common mistake so be aware of it.

"The apple's are ready to be picked." ✗

"The apples are ready to be picked." ✓

Using apostrophes correctly is essential for clear and accurate writing, as misplacement or misuse can lead to confusion or grammatical errors, as the examples below show.

i) Am I looking at my dinner or the dog's?

ii) Am I looking at my dinner or the dogs?

See the difference? The first asks whether I am looking at my dinner or the dog's dinner. The second asks whether I am looking at my dinner or looking at dogs!

Your turn.

1. Write a sentence that includes a possessive noun using apostrophe + 's'.

____

2. Write a sentence that includes a plural possessive noun that ends in 's' (e.g. 'boys').

____

3. Write a sentence that includes a contraction with an apostrophe.

____

TASK 18.

Are the following sentences correct? If not, write the correct version.

1. The dogs leash is too long.

____

2. Its a beautiful day outside.

____

3. Their going to the park tomorrow.

____

4. The boys changing room is out of order.

____

5. Hes the best at what he does.

____

6. Who's book is this?

____

7. We went to Johns' party last night.

____

8. Im looking forward to the weekends.

____

9. The swan's were flying high over the river.

____

Exclamation marks.

An exclamation mark (!) is a punctuation mark used in writing to express strong emotions, excitement, emphasis, or surprise. It is placed at the end of a sentence to indicate an exclamatory or emotional tone.

Examples:

Expressing excitement: "I can't wait to see you tonight!"

Conveying surprise: "Wow! What a beautiful sunset!"

Showing enthusiasm: "Great job on your presentation!"

Demonstrating urgency: "Hurry up! We're going to be late!"

Adding emphasis: "I absolutely love that movie!"

TASK 19.

The following are situations in which an exclamation mark could be used. Think of a suitable exclamation for each situation.

Example: Lost – "Help! I think I'm lost!"

Finding buried treasure. ______________________________

Riding a roller coaster for the first time. ______________________________

Receiving a surprise gift. ______________________________

Witnessing a meteor shower. ______________________________

Solving a difficult puzzle. ______________________________

Discovering a hidden passage. ______________________________

Meeting your favourite celebrity. ______________________________

Winning a lottery jackpot. ______________________________

Ellipse.

An ellipse (also spelled as "ellipsis") is a punctuation mark consisting of three dots (...) used to indicate missing words or a pause in a sentence. It is often used to create a sense of trailing off, leaving a thought unfinished, or to indicate that there is more information that is not stated. In stories, this can help to build tension.

Examples:

Missing words: "I went to the store and bought apples, oranges, ... and bananas."

Pause or trailing off: "Well, I'm not sure if I should... um... go to the party tonight."

Suspense or unfinished thought: "The noise came from the dark alley, and she approached, heart pounding..."

In descriptive writing the ellipse can also be used to signal a pause, to slow the reader down, which helps to emphasise a particular description. For example, in the short paragraph below, the ellipse helps to slow the reading down and so helps to emphasise the slow, relaxed nature of the scene.

"As the sun dipped below the horizon, casting a warm, golden hue across the tranquil lake... the world seemed to slow down, allowing a moment of reflection amidst the serene beauty of the evening."

Write your own paragraph that uses ellipses somewhere, either to indicate a pause, missing words, or an unfinished idea.

Hyphen & Dashes.

Hyphens.

We use a hyphen (-) to join words together or to separate the parts of a single word.

Examples:
"Mother-in-law"; "Self-esteem"; "Two-year-old"; "Well-known"; "Bird-of-prey"; "Wishy-washy"; "Check-in".

We also use hyphens to connect some prefixes and suffixes.

Examples:
"Ex-president"; "Pre-existing"; "Non-native"; "Re-enter".

Not all compound words or word combinations require hyphens, so it's best to check a dictionary if you are not sure.

Dashes.

A dash is a punctuation mark used in writing to create emphasis, separate information, or indicate a pause. Dashes are slightly longer than hyphens and have a different function. A dash is used to indicate a break in thought, or to emphasise a point. It can also be used in place of brackets or commas.

Examples:
The towering oak tree – adorned with vibrant green leaves – stood proudly as a guardian of the forest, casting a dappled, cool shadow on the lush undergrowth below.

The sunlit meadow – a sea of golden wildflowers – beckoned to weary travellers, offering a serene sanctuary amidst the rolling hills and chirping songbirds.

Putting it all together.

Read through the passage paying attention to all the instances of punctuation. Think about the effect that the punctuation has.

In the heart of the tranquil forest, sunlight filtered through the trees in a majestic dance of light and shadow; the trees, tall and ancient, stood as silent guards, their bark clothed with the wondrous carvings of time's passage. A symphony of sounds filled the air: the melodious call of birdsong; the gentle rustling of leaves; the distant, rhythmic murmur of a babbling brook – nature's magnificent orchestra. As the day drew to a close, the sky was painted with hues of pink and gold; stars began to emerge … winking like diamonds, creating a magical moment of pure wonder! Emerging from the horizon, the moon rose like a lantern, illuminating the treetops with sliver rays. Away in the distance, a mysterious howl echoed through the valley...

TASK 20.

This passage needs punctuation. Add as many different forms of punctuation as you can, making sure the punctuation is used correctly.

In the heart of the forest a symphony of natures sounds harmonised the sweet song of starlings, the gentle whispers of the wind and the babbling of the brook echoed through the valley a kaleidoscope of colours stretched out before me vibrant bluebells carpeted the meadow and a burst of reds yellows and purples fluttered as butterflies danced upon the petals like a friendly guardian the sun cast its warm embrace upon the earth its golden rays gently caressing the treetops creating a shimmering array of light and shadow how marvellous sandwiched between moss and ivy a stone path led the way up to a ruined castle still standing defiantly as a proud testimony to a former age

6. Consistent tenses.

Read the passage below and see if you can identify a problem.

> Winter is dying and spring comes to the river. Bitter, twisted branches turned leafy and luscious while infant blades of grass emerge from the frozen grime. The calm, sparkling water will soothe us. The magnificent oak tree stood proud and expectant. Hidden lives underground rustle and rumble, awakening to the music of the sparrows circling above. Lines of perfectly placed roses and daffodils danced among the magnificent coastal redwoods. Sweet waves of pine and primrose are washing over me. Like floating stars, fireflies shimmer in the twilight.

Did you find the problem? If not, look again, paying attention to the highlighted text.

> Winter is dying and spring comes to the river. Bitter, twisted branches turned leafy and luscious while infant blades of grass emerge from the frozen grime. The calm, sparkling water will soothe us. The magnificent oak tree stood proud and expectant. Hidden lives underground rustle and rumble, awakening to the music of the sparrows circling above. Lines of perfectly placed daisies and daffodils danced among the magnificent coastal redwoods. Sweet waves of pine and primrose are washing over me. Like floating stars, fireflies shimmered in the twilight.

A very common mistake that young learners make in creative writing (and all writing) is getting their tenses mixed up. For descriptive writing, the rule is simple: if you start writing in the past tense, aim to keep all the main verbs in the past tense from beginning to end. If you start in the present tense, keep it in the present tense. The passage above makes the mistake of mixing past and present tense, which can be confusing for a reader.

Key point: **Keep your tenses consistent. If you start in the past tense, keep all your main verbs in the past tense.**

TASK 21.

Read the following about Oscar's morning routine. Underline all the verbs.

At 6:30am Oscar's day begins with the sound of his alarm, and he hops out of bed with youthful energy. At 6:45, after a quick shower, he grabs a cereal bar and rushes to get dressed for school. Oscar's school bus arrives at 7:30 and he heads off for a day of learning. At school, Oscar attends classes, participates in football, and socialises with his friends during lunch breaks. At 3:30pm, once back home, Oscar completes his homework assignments and then goes out to play football.

Now re-write the passage in the past tense, beginning with "Yesterday…". The first sentence has been done for you.

Yesterday Oscar's day began with the sound of his alarm.

Re-write these sentences in the past tense:

1. They live in a big house. ______________________________
2. He walks to school every day. ______________________________
3. I eat breakfast at 7am. ______________________________
4. The sun rises in the East. ______________________________
5. We play tennis at weekend. ______________________________
6. She visits her grandmother. ______________________________
7. The train departs at 8:30am. ______________________________
8. They speak English fluently. ______________________________
9. Thc birds sing in the morning. ______________________________
10. They dream of being rich. ______________________________
11. He drives to work. ______________________________
12. I climb the mountain. ______________________________
13. The church bells ring. ______________________________
14. We swim often. ______________________________
15. She always forgets her way. ______________________________
16. Tom gives his money away. ______________________________
17. They try hard. ______________________________
18. The birds soar. ______________________________
19. They are friendly. ______________________________
20. The day is beautiful. ______________________________

TASK 22.

This passage has inconsistent tenses. Re-write it, putting the main verbs into the past tense. (The main verbs are highlighted.)

Nestled high in the rugged embrace of the mountains, a picturesque scene **will unfold** before my eyes. Towering pine trees, their dark green needles swaying gently in the breeze, **frame** the foreground of this majestic landscape. Vibrant wildflowers **carpet** the ground, offering a kaleidoscope of colours – tulips, daisies, and heather **dance** in harmony, creating a vibrant scene that **beckons** me to explore further. At the heart of this wilderness, a pristine alpine lake **glistens** in the midday sun, its waters mirroring the azure sky above. A crystal-clear stream **feeds** the lake, its gentle babbling providing a soothing soundtrack to this natural sanctuary. Above, the sun **will hang** like a radiant jewel in a flawless sapphire sky, casting a warm, golden glow over the entire scene. As I **look** up, I **have spotted** eagles soaring with effortless grace, their powerful wings painting lazy circles in the endless azure sky above.

7. Show don't tell.

You may have heard your teacher say "Show don't tell" before. It is a phrase that English teachers are very fond of repeating when teaching learners how to write well. It's an important technique for creative writing, yet is one of the most difficult to master. So, what exactly does "show don't tell" mean?

The best way to demonstrate "show don't tell" is with an example.

 = bad

 = good

"It was a really hot day". ← **Tell** 

That's a statement that simply ***tells*** the reader something about the day. It simply states a fact, rather than describing it. However, what about if we don't *tell* the reader it's a hot day, but rather ***show*** it's a hot day by describing some of the effects of the hot weather.

Consider this:

"The temperature was rocketing, and sweat was pouring off his brow. Steam was rising off the lake, and the tarmac on the road was beginning to melt." ← **Show** 

Do you see the difference? We have practically said it's a hot day WITHOUT ACTUALLY USING THE WORDS "hot day". We have described some of the typical effects of a hot day and allowed the reader to imagine or infer what this means. This is showing, not telling. Let's consider some more examples:

"Telling" is factual and avoids detail; "showing" is detailed and aims to transport the reader into the scene being described.

TELL 	**SHOW** 
The bedroom was messy.	"A mountain of clothes was piled up against the wall. Weeks-old takeaway cartons and coke bottles littered the floor. Dust and grime coated the windowpanes. Countless pieces of crumpled up paper lay across the bed."
The garden was beautiful. It had a lovely smell.	The flowers were in full bloom; their scarlet and emerald petals brought the garden to life. The sweet smell of lilac and pine washed over me and beckoned me further into this miniature paradise.
It was frosty and cold outside.	The ice-coated floor sparkled like a carpet of crystals as the bitter, arctic wind stung every sinew.
The man was very nervous.	The man was biting his nails and shifting around in his seat. Sweat was beginning to form on his forehead.

So, by "showing", we are painting a scene with more vivid, sensory details rather than merely stating facts. And by doing this, the writing becomes richer and more meaningful; you allow your reader to *experience* objects, events and situations.

"Don't tell me the moon is shining. Show me the glint of light on broken glass."

Anton Chekhov.

'Show don't tell' in famous literature.

Many of the best writers use 'show don't tell'. Below are a few examples. As you read them, take note of the writers' techniques; underline or highlight interesting descriptions.

The Secret Garden, by Frances Hodgson Burnett.

"The rainstorm had ended and the gray mist and clouds had been swept away in the night by the wind. The wind itself had ceased and a brilliant, deep blue sky arched high over the moorland. Never, never had Mary dreamed of a sky so blue. In India skies were hot and blazing; this was of a deep cool blue which almost seemed to sparkle like the waters of some lovely bottomless lake, and here and there, high, high in the arched blueness floated small clouds of snow-white fleece. The far-reaching world of the moor itself looked softly blue instead of gloomy purple-black or awful dreary gray."

Kew Gardens, by Virginia Woolf.

"From the oval shaped flowerbed there rose perhaps a hundred stalks spreading into heart-shaped or tongue-shaped leaves half way up and unfurling at the tip red or blue or yellow petals marked with spots of colour raised upon the surface; and from the red, blue or yellow gloom of the throat emerged a straight bar, rough with gold dust and slightly clubbed at the end. The petals were voluminous enough to be stirred by the summer breeze, and when they moved, the red, blue and yellow lights passed one over the other, staining an inch of the brown earth beneath with a spot of the most intricate colour."

Oliver Twist, by Charles Dickens.

"A dirtier or more wretched place he had never seen. The street was very narrow and muddy, and the air was impregnated with filthy odours. There were a good many small shops; but the only stock in trade appeared to be heaps of children, who, even at that time of night, were crawling in and out at the doors, or screaming from the inside."

The Two Towers, by J. R. R. Tolkien.

"The gasping pools were choked with ash and crawling muds, sickly white and grey, as if the mountains had vomited the filth of their entrails upon the lands about. High mounds of crushed and powdered rock, great cones of earth fire-blasted and poison-stained, stood like an obscene graveyard in endless rows, slowly revealed in the reluctant light."

TASK 23.

Change the "tell" sentences into "show" sentences adding as much detail as possible.

Tell: The temperature fell, and it started to snow.

Show: ____

____

____

____

Tell: The garden looked beautiful and smelled so sweet.

Show: ____

____

____

____

Tell: The man was old and looked tired.

Show: ____

____

____

____

Tell: The hurricane had destroyed the town.

Show: ____

____

____

____

Tell: It was night time. The castle was creepy.

Show: ____

____

____

____

Tell: The city was very busy with people.
There were lots of sounds and smells.

Show: ____

____

____

____

Tell: The lake was beautiful.

Show: ____

____

____

____

____

Tell: The room was abandoned and filthy.

Show: ____

____

____

____

Tell: Miriam was very sad.

Show: ____

____

____

____

8. Engaging the five senses.

Powerful description needs to be sensuous. By appealing to the reader's senses the writer can help the reader to experience the scene much more vividly and realistically. In your writing you should aim to engage as many of the five senses as possible. Look at the picture below. Brainstorm as many things that you can see, hear, smell etc. as possible. Use your imagination to add extra details.

What can I see? (List 10 things)

What can I hear? (List 5 things)

What can I smell? (List 3 things)

What can I taste? (List 1 thing)

What can I feel? (List 3 things)

Sight (Vision): Visual imagery helps us to paint pictures with words, like describing a lush green forest, a vibrant red sunset, or a sparkling blue ocean. It helps readers see the world you're creating in their minds. When creating visual imagery, think not only about objects, but shapes, colours, sizes, patterns, light and shadow.

Brainstorm things you can see.
colours: pink, rouge, emerald, forest-green, golden, silver, sapphire,
shapes: arches, lines, circular, straight
shadow pillars, petals, shrubs, path,
sky, clouds, sunlight, birds

Layers of exquisite greenery lined the walkway, mixed with gentle pinks, crimson and gold. Soft strips of light fell through the rose-adorned archway, illuminating and warming the silver path. Columns of shade stretched across the floor like Roman soldiers, while pink petals floated to the floor like delicate angels. Small, circular shrubs stood either side of the path guiding the way into the darker, cooler wood. Above, a golden sun radiated down as fluffy clouds – like balls of cotton-wool – drifted across a serene, sapphire sky.

Included in the above description are not just objects, but a variety of visual items such as shapes (arch, circular), shades of light (light vs darker), colours, patterns (lines and strips). Also included are items that are not directly visible from the picture, but which we know would be there (e.g. sky, sun, clouds). Use the imagination to bring more items into your picture.

Hearing (Auditory): Think of the crunch of leaves in the forest, the soft purring of a cat, or the roar of a crowd at a sports game. Sounds make your writing come alive and can set the mood. When describing sounds, remember, do not just think about all the obvious sounds that might be included in the visual frame of the picture. Use your imagination to think of additional things. Read the example below and highlight or underline any sound-related words. Look at page 131 for an answer.

Brainstorm things you can hear.
bees, birds, wind, water running, dog barking, children playing, distant noises, cars or planes / trains, people talking, leaves rustling

An orchestra of worker bees buzzed and hummed their way around the hibiscus and honeysuckle, accompanied by a lively choir of sparrows and starlings above. As the water fountain continued its ceaseless splashing and chattering, a tranquil breeze whispered through the vines: the serenity was disturbed only by the occasional yelps of a nearby dog or the faint whir of a distant jet plane.

Notice, there is no water visible in the garden picture, or any airplanes, but we have used our imagination to create their sounds. Imagining additional things, which are outside the immediate visual field, gives you more opportunities to show off your descriptive skills. What you can see in the image is only your starting point. You are expected to use your imagination to fill in the gaps.

Smell (Olfactory): Smell descriptions can transport readers to different places and times. You can write about the fresh scent of rain, the delicious aroma of baking bread, or the salty sea breeze. Smells can trigger memories and emotions.

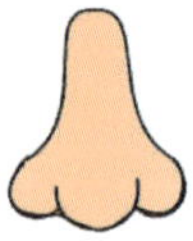

Brainstorm things you can smell.

At the opening of the path, subtle waves of pine and primrose and petunia washed over me, like the perfume of paradise. As I ventured further along a more intense aroma of oakwood and freshly cut grass began to emerge.

Other scents might include: barbecue, grilled sweetcorn or other foods; coffee; wood burning; farmyard smells; leather; earth or soil; dried leaves; apple trees; moss. Remember to describe the ***quality*** of the smell too, using words such as intense, subtle, fresh, stale, acrid, pungent, sharp. See page 131 for more ideas.

Due to its close association with memory, the sense of smell can be a good trigger for flashback. A flashback is where you recall something from the past. For example, the scent of the roses can be used to take you back to childhood. You can then use this flashback as a way to bring in new descriptions based on imagination. We will say more about this under taste (below).

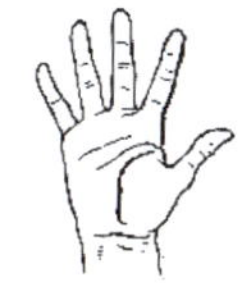

Touch (Tactile): Describing how something feels helps readers connect with your writing. Is it soft like a fluffy pillow, rough like tree bark, or icy like a snowflake? Touch descriptions make your writing more relatable.

Brainstorm things suggesting touch.

Soft, balmy currents of sun-kissed air stroked my face. A grainy path extended before me. Delicate, emerald leaves enveloped the path like a satin cloak. Bristles and thorns mingled with smooth, silky petals. Directly ahead stood a proud ancient oak: solid as steel. The gentle sound of running water sent tingles down my spine. Furry, forest-green moss crawled up the oak's rigid body, while its tired, wrinkly arms still provide a home to countless lifeforms.

Do not describe only things you can directly touch, but how things could or would feel *if* you touched them. For example, in our garden picture, you might only be touching the path under your feet and nothing else. But you can still describe the imagined texture of the flowers, leaves, trees, water, etc., without actually touching them.

You can also describe the physical effects on your body of something related to one of the other senses. For example, I might ***see*** a huge, hairy spider, and that might make my <u>skin crawl</u>. Or I might hear the sweet sound of starlings, and that might <u>send tingles</u> down my spine!

Remember, whatever your scene, there will always be temperature, whether this is caused directly by the effects of the weather (the sun or icy wind burning your skin), the fire inside a house (warming your toes) or some other cause.

Taste (Gustatory): Even though we can't taste words, describing flavours and tastes adds depth to your writing. You can talk about the sweetness of chocolate, the tanginess of a lemon, or the saltiness of the sea.

Brainstorm things suggesting taste.

In the vibrant garden the gentle breeze carried with it the aroma of sun-warmed earth and fresh herbs. Wandering further, lush basil leaves released their peppery embrace, and nearby, the sweet vines of ripe strawberries hung low. The air itself tasted of freedom, preparing me for the flavours waiting to be discovered among the thriving herbs and fruits.

! tip Smell and taste are closely related, so turn smells into tastes or focus on smells that can also be tastes. For example, "sweet", "sour", "bitter", "smoky", "salty", all of these can be smells ***and*** tastes. By calling the roses "sweet" or the smell of trash "sour", you are already evoking taste.

! tip Use flashbacks. Flashbacks, involving memories of tastes, can be triggered by other senses. For example, the smell of apple trees can trigger a memory of homemade apple pie, or a sound of music can trigger a memory of when you were a young child, lying in your grandparents' garden, with the smell of freshly-baked bread coming from the kitchen. The ***smell*** of freshly baked bread evokes the ***taste*** of freshly-baked bread.

9. Devices and techniques.

Descriptive writing needs SHAMPOO to make it sparkle and shine. SHAMPOO stands for Similes, Hyperbole, Alliteration, Metaphor, Personification, Onomatopoeia and Openings. Before we start with this, let's test your current knowledge.

TASK 24.

See if you can identify one of each of the following language devices in the passage below.

Simile ____

Hyperbole ____

Alliteration ____

Metaphor ____

Personification ____

Onomatopoeia ____

In the heart of the garden, nature's symphony played its morning chorus. The sun stretched its golden arms over the petals, persuading them to unfurl like drowsy dancers. Roses, radiant in their scarlet gowns, danced with glee, while millions upon millions of daffodils whispered their secrets in the hushed breeze. The garden's path, like a ribbon of dreams, wound through this floral wonderland. Beneath the ancient oak's wise branches, the moss-carpeted earth told a thousand stories. Butterflies, the garden's confetti, fluttered in joy. Bees buzzed and hummed in harmonious conversation, while the leaves above rustled in applause.

Similes.

When we compare one thing with another thing using "like" or "as" we call that a simile. Similes are a form of imagery that make your writing more engaging and more interesting. Similes help to emphasise a particular feature of a thing or person and help the reader to get a more vivid picture in their mind.

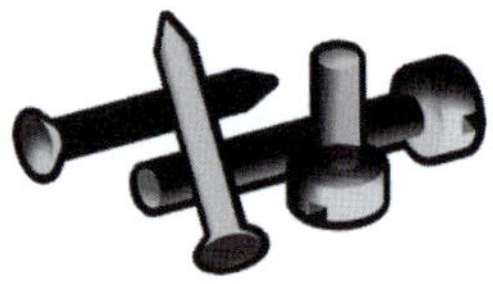

The Ninja was as hard as nails.

His house creaked like an old ship.

Below there are three similes from famous writers. Do some research and see if you can find out who wrote them.

Writer's name.

"I wandered lonely as a cloud" ______________________________

"Old Marley was as dead as a doornail." ______________________________

"As constant as the northern star." ______________________________

When you use similes avoid using ones which are too obvious, common or basic. Aim to use a simile that's original or unusual, though not so unusual that it loses all meaning.

As cold as ice (common simile).
As cold as a rug (meaningless simile)
As cold as a polar blast (effective and original simile)

"He lingered like a bad smell" is a common simile. We could change it to something more original, such as "He lingered like a dead skunk around my neck."

TASK 25.

Think of a suitable word or phrase to complete these similes.

As ______________________ as an old boot.

As ______________________ as a sardine.

As ______________________ as a dart.

As ______________________ as a sword.

As ______________________ as a sleepy sloth.

As ______________________ as reinforced steel.

As ______________________ as a sleeping baby.

As ______________________ as a sapphire.

As ______________________ as a carpet of crystals.

As ______________________ as a fireball.

As light as ______________________________

As stubborn as ___________________________

She moved as gracefully as __________________________

His laughter was as melodious as ________________________

TASK 26.

Complete these similes with a suitable word or phrase.

The moon looked like ______________________________

I rolled out of bed like ______________________________

The lake was like ______________________________

The house was like ______________________________

The sky was like ______________________________

The clouds were like ______________________________

It was so hot it was like ______________________________

It was so cold it was like ______________________________

The night was as black as ______________________________

Wrinkles covered the man's face like ___________________________

The movie was so boring it was like ______________________________

I leapt across the floor like ____________________________

I sped off like ______________________________

His smile lit up the room like ___________________________

Metaphors.

Like similes, metaphors are a form of imagery. They also aim to highlight certain features of a thing or person by comparing it with something else. However, unlike similes, metaphors do not use "like" or "as" for comparison; they compare things directly by stating that a thing ***is*** another thing, rather than just similar to it.

Similes.	Metaphors.
He is like a breath of fresh air.	**He is a breath of fresh air.**
She is as fast as a tiger.	**She is a tiger when she runs.**
Jack's heart is like gold.	**Jack has a heart of gold.**

He's the light of my life.

He's a real couch potato.

He's a walking dictionary.

She's a star pupil.

TASK 27.

Read each example below. Choose whether you think it's a simile or a metaphor and then explain what two things are being compared.

Example: Love is the compass of the heart.

This is an example of: simile / metaphor

What is being compared?
Love is being compared to a compass

1. The sky was like a sapphire quilt.

This is an example of: simile / metaphor

What is being compared?

2. Her tears were a river of sorrow.

This is an example of: simile / metaphor

What is being compared?

3. Time is a thief in the night.

This is an example of: simile / metaphor

What is being compared?

4. His anger was like a volcano waiting to erupt.

This is an example of: simile / metaphor

What is being compared?

TASK 28.

Below are lots of words and phrases which can be made into metaphors. Use the words to try to produce at least 10 metaphors by mixing and matching.

Example Hope | Light in the darkness

Metaphor: Hope is a light in the darkness.

Love | Bridge built over time | Her smile | Salma | Rollercoaster

Laughter | Zoo | Blanket on a cold winter night | Bottomless pit

Flies | Snow-covered field | Blanket of diamonds | Life | Trust

Billy | Carpet of diamonds | Night sky | Journey | Breath of fresh air

Jim's stomach | Music of the soul | Time | Ray of sunshine | Ideas

Heart of gold | River flowing endlessly | Night owl | Classroom

Knowledge | Beacon of light in darkness

Metaphor: ______________________________

Metaphor: ______________________________

Metaphor: ______________________________

Metaphor: ______________________________

Metaphor: ______________________________

Metaphor: ______________________________

Metaphor: ______________________________

Metaphor: ______________________________

Metaphor: ______________________________

Alliteration.

Alliteration involves the repetition of sounds across several different words which are close to each other. For example, **P**eter **P**iper **p**icked a **p**eck of **p**ickled **p**epper is an example of alliteration because it repeats the initial "p" sound multiple times throughout the line.

Strictly speaking, alliteration relates only to the *initial* sound of a word (usually the first letter) and should involve only consonant sounds (not vowels). However, there are other forms of alliteration that apply to vowels rather than consonants as well as sounds that occur anywhere else in the word and not just the initial sound at the beginning of a word. For example, *consonance* is a form of alliteration that relates to the repetition of a consonant sound (e.g., 'f') anywhere in the sentence.

"**Ph**ilip is terri**f**ied of rou**gh** bu**ff**oons." Notice the consonance relates to sounds, not letters. Both 'ph' and 'ough' generate 'f' sounds and so it is the 'f' ***sound*** that is alliterated.

Another type of alliteration is assonance. This relates to vowels rather than consonants. "H**ey**, w**ai**t L**a**dy J**a**ne!" Yet another form of alliteration is sibilance. This is the repeated use of the "s" or "sh" sound to generate a hissing quality, as in "The slimy snake slithered down the slope".

Why do we use alliteration?

We use alliteration to give writing a lyrical or more emotive effect. It also helps the writing to stand out making it more memorable and more impactful. For example, "the little old lady" sounds much better than "the aged old woman". We can also use alliteration to echo sounds associated with the thing we are describing. For example, "the splashing, silver stream" uses alliteration to generate a hissing sound that might be created by a fast-running stream. This can help the reader to form a more vivid image of what is being described.

Task 29.

Read the poem below by Edgar Allen Poe and underline as many instances of alliteration that you can find.

The Raven

Once upon a midnight dreary, while I pondered, weak and weary,
Over many a quaint and curious volume of forgotten lore—
While I nodded, nearly napping, suddenly there came a tapping,
As of some one gently rapping, rapping at my chamber door.
"'Tis some visitor," I muttered, "tapping at my chamber door—
Only this and nothing more."

Ah, distinctly I remember it was in the bleak December;
And each separate dying ember wrought its ghost upon the floor.
Eagerly I wished the morrow;—vainly I had sought to borrow
From my books surcease of sorrow—sorrow for the lost Lenore—
For the rare and radiant maiden whom the angels name Lenore—
Nameless here for evermore.

And the silken, sad, uncertain rustling of each purple curtain
Thrilled me—filled me with fantastic terrors never felt before;
So that now, to still the beating of my heart, I stood repeating
"'Tis some visitor entreating entrance at my chamber door—
Some late visitor entreating entrance at my chamber door;—
This it is and nothing more."

Presently my soul grew stronger; hesitating then no longer,
"Sir," said I, "or Madam, truly your forgiveness I implore;
But the fact is I was napping, and so gently you came rapping,
And so faintly you came tapping, tapping at my chamber door,
That I scarce was sure I heard you"—here I opened wide the door;—
Darkness there and nothing more.

Hyperbole.

Hyperbole is the use of exaggeration for special effect. It is a common device that we often use in everyday speech without realising it. For example, you may have heard your teacher say "I've told you a million times" or your parent say "Hurry up! I've been waiting ages." You might have sat in a boring English lesson and thought to yourself "This lesson is going on forever!" or you might have felt so hungry that you "could eat a horse". All of these are common examples of hyperbole.

TASK 30.

Complete these sentences with suitably hyperbolic words or phrases.

1. The building was so big it was practically ____________________

2. I was so tired, I slept like a _________________________

3. The journey was so long. It seemed to last _____________________

4. I'm so busy, I have ____________________ things to do

5. He's skinnier than a ______________________

6. She cried _________________________

7. I have to go to the shop but I'll be back in _____________________

8. That is the most beautiful dress in the __________________

9. You are in England and someone says: "She was screaming so loud, you could hear her ________________________"

10. I was so embarrassed I nearly ______________________

11. You are the best friend in the ____________________

12. That racing car was so fast it was gone in ____________________

Onomatopoeia.

Have you heard of onomatopoeia? It's a big word, but it's not as hard as it seems! Onomatopoeia is when we use words that sound like the things they describe. Like when we say 'meow,' it sounds just like the noise a cat makes, and 'woof' sounds like the sound a dog makes.

There are many other onomatopoeic words, such as 'bang,' 'crash,' 'smash,' 'plop,' 'wham,' 'pitter-patter,' and 'clap.' When we use these words, it makes the story or description more exciting because they appeal to our sense of sound. So, onomatopoeia is a fun way to make stories more interesting by using words that sound like the actions or sounds they describe!

TASK 31.

Underline all the examples of onomatopoeia in the sentences below.

- The windows rattled in their frames, creating an eerie symphony of sound.
- The distant boom of explosions echoed through the valley.
- The peace was disturbed by the clattering of cups and plates coming from the kitchen.
- The glass shattered when he rested his cup on it.
- Sizzling sweetcorn hissed on the crackling campfire as the wind whirred over the trees.
- All around, the air was filled with the soft music of buzzing bees and chirping birds.
- The thunder rumbled loudly in the distance as the storm approached.
- The bees buzzed around the colourful garden, collecting nectar from the flowers.
- The baby giggled with delight as the puppy's tail thumped against the floor.
- The sizzling bacon in the frying pan made my mouth water.
- The old floorboards creaked underfoot as we tiptoed through the haunted house.

TASK 32.

Now see if you can make your own sentences using onomatopoeia with the words below. You can change the tense of the word if needed. For example,

Word: "hiss". **Sentence:** The snake hissed as it slid down the path.

rattle boom clatter shattered sizzle crackle whirr whisper creak rustle bang beep

Sentence one: ______________________________

____

Sentence two: ______________________________

____

Sentence three: ______________________________

____

Sentence four: ______________________________

____

Sentence five: ______________________________

____

Sentence six: ______________________________

____

rattle boom clatter shattered sizzle crackle whirr whisper creak rustle bang beep

Sentence seven: ____________________

____

Sentence eight: ____________________

____

Sentence nine: ____________________

____

Sentence ten: ____________________

____

Sentence eleven: ____________________

____

Sentence twelve: ____________________

____

Openers.

"Openings" refers not simply to the way you begin your description, but also the openings of each and every paragraph or sentence. The most common way to begin sentences is with a noun. For example:

The house was amazing!

A river rushed through the valley.

The daffodils looked like a million suns.

Clouds were floating in the majestic sky.

I could hear bells ringing.

English is a subject-verb-object language, so it is normal to begin with a noun or noun phrase, because nouns form the subject of the sentence. However, in creative writing it becomes boring if you begin every sentence in the same way. Creative writing is supposed to be original and unusual, not boring and repetitive. Read the passage below:

> I am on a journey to a distant place. I set off with nothing but my map and a compass. I meander through the village, where cute cottages and exquisite hedgerows line the way. I smell sweet aromas coming from the gardens and musical sounds coming from the sky above where the sparrows hover. The road takes me over a fast-flowing river and through a deep, grassy valley. The sun is dripping heat and the sky is smiling. The wind gently strokes my face. The place reminds me of my childhood. I am happy to be here.

Do you see anything wrong with the passage above? It is actually well written and descriptive. It appeals to different senses (sight, smell, sound, touch) and uses a simile and a metaphor. However, each sentence opens either with "I" + verb, or a noun (preceded by an article 'The'). This is boring and leads to a sense of monotony throughout the writing. It needs to be changed. There are many other ways to open a sentence without a noun or a pronoun and you should aim to experiment with different types of openers.

Opening with a VERB:

Looking up at the sky, I knew a storm was coming.

Towering over the valley, the mountain was a sight to behold.

Opening with an ADJECTIVE:

Cute cottages and exquisite hedgerows lined the way.

Excited, I jumped for joy.

Opening with an ADVERB:

Cautiously, I took a bite.

Ominously, ravens circled in the sky above.

Opening with a SIMILE:

Like an anaconda, the snaky river meandered through the valley.

As bright as a thousand suns, the sunflowers shone in the valley.

Opening with a PREPOSITION:

On top of the hill was a lighthouse.

After the storm, all was calm.

Opening with a CONJUNCTION:

But it was a spectacular sight.

And the wind whispered through the valley.

Opening with a PARTICIPIAL PHRASE:

Covered in a layer of fresh, powdery snow, the hills beckoned.

Excited by the unexpected snowfall, the children rushed outside.

TASK 33.

Re-write the paragraph below using a range of different openers, including verbs, adjectives, adverbs, prepositions and similes.

I am on a journey to a distant place. I set off with nothing but my map and a compass. I meander through the village, where cute cottages and exquisite hedgerows line the way. I smell sweet aromas coming from the gardens like the perfume of paradise, while music echoes from the sky above where the sparrows hover. Lanes, so charming, take me over fast-flowing rivers and through deep, grassy valleys. The sun is dripping heat above and the sky is smiling. The wind gently strokes my face.

10. Pan & Zoom (AKA Zoom in Zoom out).

In writing, "pan and zoom" is a descriptive technique that allows the writer to focus on specific details or elements of a scene while maintaining a broader perspective. This technique is used in cinema, where a camera can pan (move horizontally) or zoom (adjust the zoom to magnify or shrink the view) to highlight certain aspects. When applied to writing, "pan and zoom" involves shifting the focus from a wide view of the surroundings to a more detailed examination of a specific object, character, or action within that scene. This helps to create a vivid and immersive experience for the reader by guiding their attention and emphasising important elements. Here's an example of how "pan and zoom" might be used in descriptive writing:

Original Passage (Wide View): "The cityscape stretched out before them, a sprawling metropolis of towering skyscrapers, bustling streets, and a river winding through its heart."

Using "Pan and Zoom": "The cityscape stretched out before them, a sprawling metropolis of towering skyscrapers, bustling streets, and a river winding through its heart. As their eyes followed the river's meandering path, they focused in on a charming café nestled along the water's edge. The aroma of freshly brewed coffee wafted from its open windows, inviting passersby to indulge in a moment of relaxation amidst the urban hustle."

In this example, the initial description sets the stage with a wide view of the cityscape. The writer then directs the reader's attention (zooms in) to a specific detail—the café—and provides a closer, more detailed look at it. This technique helps paint a more vivid picture and engages the reader's senses by focusing on specific sensory details, such as the aroma of coffee.

The garden is a paradise of colours with life unfolding before your eyes. Stepping into this vibrant place, the senses are flooded by the kaleidoscope of blooms and the soothing harmony of nature's music. Wildflowers sway gently in the breeze, an array of lilacs, pinks, and golds. Fluttering and humming among the blossoms, bees and butterflies are joined by a choir of starlings, parading in the sapphire sky.

To the left, a sunflower, bathed in the warm, golden glow of the sun, stands tall and majestic in a sea of lush green: its face is a glorious display of nature's wonder. The sunflower's large, round head forms a pattern of deep, buttery-yellow petals that radiate outward from a central, dark chocolate-brown disk. Like delicate eyelashes, each petal has a soft, velvety texture, with fringed edges. Their surfaces catch the sunlight, creating a shimmering halo of brilliance, as the sweet fragrance of pollen fills the air.

Hovering near the sunflower's face is a diligent bee, darting in and out of the flowers like a skilled acrobat in search of treasure. In this enchanting dance, the bee and the sunflower form a graceful partnership, a symbol of nature's harmony.

11. Scaffolds & Samples.

You never know what you will be asked to create a description of in your exam. It could be a garden scene, a mountain scene, a desert, a house, a beach, a storm, or something else. However, if you start to develop and memorise descriptions of some of the most common things, this will help you to do well in the test no matter what picture you get. Some of the most common things include:

- Weather
- A building
- A person
- A nature scene

Weather.

The weather provides lots of opportunities for great descriptions. It can be good or bad weather, or both. Weather can include rain, snow, sleet; gentle, whispering winds; gusty, howling winds; sunshine, clouds, thunder, lightning, fog, tornadoes, storms, hailstone, etc. Each of these can be described in countless ways, using different colours and devices.

Bad weather.

Lightning was threatening the fluffy silverish clouds; it flashed sharp and bright – so blinding that the sky for an instant became a single sheet of white. Like a cannon shot through the valley, a low thump of thunder echoed across the vast quilt of sky. Rolling in from the west, a thick blanket of rain cloud threatened to release floods of water onto the crowds below. Howling winds screamed through gaps in the rocks, bullying everything in its path. Freezing and drenched, a lone man took cover as the storm battered down. Luckily, I glanced across and was able to see and enormous coal-black coat hanging alone from a hungry door. I sheltered within its warmth.

Good weather.

The storm clouds steadily faded. Suddenly, everything was transformed. A radiant sun smiled from behind pink, cotton-candy clouds and the majestic sky quickly revealed its true colours: sparkling sapphire and azure. Softening into a whisper, the warm breeze gently caressed the corn fields and the conifers. Gliding in from the west were scores of elegant and graceful swans and other birds – like precious angels floating on the soft crystal-clear waters. Above, an exquisite choir of hummingbirds sang while an orchestra of bees buzzed their way through the sunflowers. The air was filled with the sweet aroma of honeysuckle and hibiscus.

Buildings.

Whatever your description is, nine times out of ten there will either be a building of some sort, or you can imagine one. Buildings can include barns, old houses, modern houses, a castle, a school, a factory, shop, library, church and more.

Appearing through a clearing in the dark, dense forest was an ancient and dilapidated house. Inside the miserable, half-ruined construction was a jewel of a room - an almost perfectly preserved library of books. Sandwiched between moss and mould, the books looked depressed as they clung to hungry-looking shelves from. Amidst the decay there was a distinct aroma of antique furniture that took me back to my childhood - to lazy days lying on my grandmother's old sheepskin rug, comforted by her reassuring voice, and the taste of freshly baked bread.

People.

People come in a wonderful wide variety of different colours, shapes and sizes, which provides you with plenty of opportunities to create varied and interesting descriptions. You can focus on facial features (eyes, ears, nose, mouth), bodily features (shoulders, arms, hands, fingers, fingernails, legs, feet), height, build, hair, clothes, voice and posture. Make sure to include as much detail as you can.

The man's weathered face told a thousand stories. Well-worn wrinkles etched into his face like deep crevasses carved into the surrounding landscape – each one suggesting its own unique chapter: some happy and hopeful, others filled with despair. Facial hair clung to the man's skin as if it were frightened to let go, frightened to reveal the truth of what lay beneath it. The thin, grassy hair on his head, however, had already given up the fight and was in retreat. Hinting at deeper mysteries buried away in his soul, his eyes expressed both wisdom and sadness. He wasn't a big man, but his presence still expressed authority and firmness. His posture, slightly stooped, spoke of the burdens he had carried and the years he had gracefully embraced.

Old and worn, his clothes hung from his shoulders, like the tired, ancient armour of a once-important knight. A thick, slate-grey winter-coat enveloped his torso, while his legs – two solid tree trunks – were comfortably encased inside shiny leather boots which were as black as the night. On his hands were tatty, woollen gloves that only covered up to his knuckles. Sharp, steely fingers popped out of the ends, like medieval lances ready for the joust.

Nature scene.

Finally, your nature scene could include a description of mountains, lakes, rivers, waterfalls, forests, a beach, an ocean, gardens and more.

Radiant sunshine was beaming down on the soft, sandy shores which stretched into the distance as far as the eye could see. Smooth sand was interrupted only by the occasional palm tree that extended upwards like a lush, emerald beacon. The glistening, golden beach caressed my feet as I lay tranquil in this unspoilt paradise. Blissful and content, I gazed out at the cobalt ocean - its gentle waves lapping against the land, dancing around the sand in joyful, rhythmic cycles. The sleepy sea began to bustle and thrive with life, while above, seagulls were soaring and swooping. Out at sea, one could see fishing boats bobbing around lazily while windsurfers coasted gracefully across the silver crests of the waves. To the west, majestic mountains touched the cyan sky, proudly protecting the valleys and plains below. Happily, I inhaled the fresh sea-salt air and could taste the freedom of this island.

Descriptive words for describing nature scenes.

Graceful	Stunning	Pristine	Majestic
Tranquil	Serene	Uninhabited	Wild
Undiscovered	Rugged	Picturesque	Breathtaking
Grand	Serene	Formidable	Magnificent
Awesome	Snow-capped	Timeless	Vast
Spectacular	Radiant	Mysterious	Gorgeous
Alluring	Elegant	Unspoiled	Solitary
Tropical	Towering	Idyllic	Jagged
Captivating	Exquisite	Sublime	Enchanting

TASK 34.

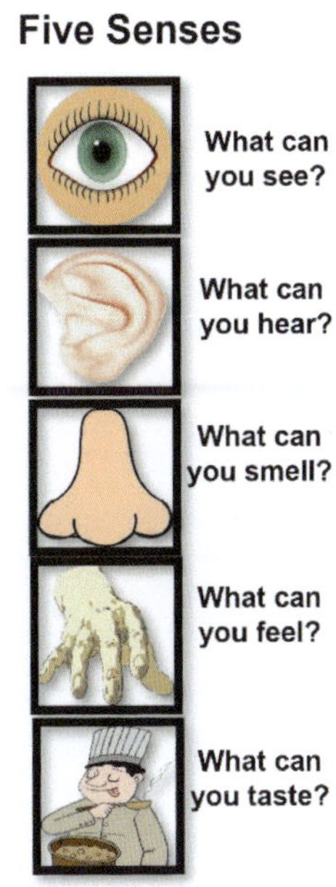

Write a description suggested by this picture. Your description should add **ten to twelve sentences.** Use a minimum of **four forms of punctuation**. Try to use the following words somewhere in your description: **gothic**, **charcoal**, **cranking**, **screeches**, **malevolent**, **chilling**, **bestial**, **howls**, **sinister**, **stench**, **rotten**. Use a minimum of **four linguistic devices** (e.g., onomatopoeia, alliteration, metaphor, simile, personification). Use **strong, descriptive verbs, adjective and adverbs**. Aim to use five senses. Make sure you **plan it first and check at the end**.

12. Narrative Writing.

Narrative writing is a form of creative writing that involves telling a story. Narrative writing includes descriptive writing, and so all the elements you have learned up to this point from the previous sections of this book are important for narrative writing too. However, narrative writing includes elements that are not included in pure descriptive writing. In the test, you could be asked either to write a description or a narrative, so you have to be prepared for both.

In this section we cover some of the elements you need in order to write effective narrative. This includes:

- Plot (including beginning, middle, end, and conflict or challenges)
- Setting
- Characters
- Narrative tension
- Narrative perspective
- Dialogue

Plot.

The first thing that narrative needs is a plot. The plot of a story refers to the sequence of events that make up the narrative; it is essential for creating tension, suspense, and engagement in a story, guiding the reader through a series of events that lead to a satisfying conclusion. Plot includes the storyline, the main events, conflicts, and resolutions that drive the story forward and shape its outcome. The plot is the framework that organises the events of a story, providing structure and coherence to the narrative. It typically includes elements such as exposition (introduction of characters and setting), rising action (development of conflict), climax (the turning point or peak of the story), falling action (resolution of the conflict), and conclusion (final outcome or resolution).

Look at the examples below. The first contains descriptions but no plot. The second has descriptions and a plot.

No plot

In the whimsical kingdom of Quirklandia, there ruled a merry monarch known far and wide as King Quirkington. His days were filled with laughter and jest and he delighted in organising parties and events for his subjects. King Quirkington's palace was a marvel of spectacular architecture. Its turrets were adorned with oversized hats, and the courtyard was a maze of quirky sculptures. The throne room, instead of a traditional throne, featured a colossal beanbag chair, where the king held court with a fake wand that glowed in the dark.

Plot

In the grand kingdom of Quirkington, the king ruled with wisdom and benevolence. One fateful night, his prized jewel, the Enigma Crown, vanished without a trace. Whispers of a shadowy thief circulated the court, casting an eerie spell over the castle. Determined to unveil the mystery, the king enlisted his most trusted advisor, Lady Big Nose. Together, they navigated the labyrinthine corridors, chasing the elusive phantom. As dawn broke, the sun revealed the crown atop the highest tower, and the court jester was smiling a knowing smile from head to toe. The kingdom breathed a sigh of relief, but the jester was imprisoned for 20 years.

A plot usually involves a central character – the protagonist – facing challenges that need to be overcome or puzzles to be solved. The plot will have a beginning, a middle and an end will normally follow the pyramidal structure below.

Plot Pyramid.

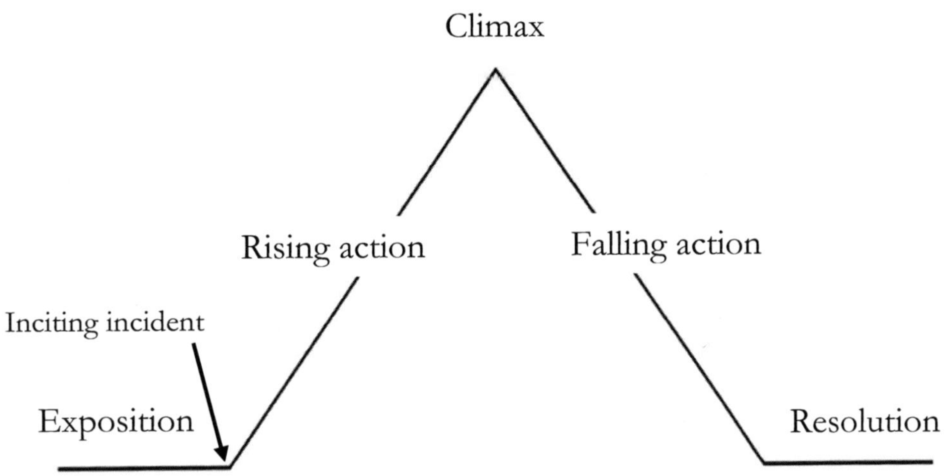

The plot pyramid is a visual representation of the main components of a narrative. The main components include:

Introduction/Exposition:

- Description: This is the beginning of the story where the setting, characters, and initial situation are introduced.
- Purpose: Establishes the context, background, and the normal state of affairs. It introduces the main characters, the setting, and any relevant information needed to understand the story.

Inciting Incident:

- Description: This is the event that disrupts the normal state of affairs and sets the story in motion.
- Purpose: Creates tension or conflict and motivates the characters to take action. It propels the story forward by introducing a problem or challenge.

Rising Action:

- Description: This phase involves a series of events that build upon the inciting incident, escalating the tension.
- Purpose: Develops the plot, introduces complications, and deepens the conflict. Characters face obstacles, make choices, and take actions that drive the story forward.

Climax:

- Description: This is the turning point or the highest point of tension in the story.
- Purpose: The central conflict reaches its peak, and the main character confronts the most significant challenge or makes a crucial decision. The outcome of the story often hinges on this moment.

Falling Action:

- Description: Events that follow the climax, resolving the main conflict.
- Purpose: Tensions ease, loose ends are tied up, and the story moves towards resolution. Characters deal with the aftermath of the climax and begin to reach closure.

Resolution:

- Description: The final part of the story where remaining questions are answered, and the narrative concludes.
- Purpose: Provides closure and reveals the ultimate fate of the characters. It may also leave room for interpretation or suggest possibilities for the future.

The plot pyramid is a useful tool for understanding the narrative structure of a story. It helps writers organise their plots, create tension, and guide the audience through a journey of conflict, resolution, and meaning.

Plot structure – Three Little Pigs.

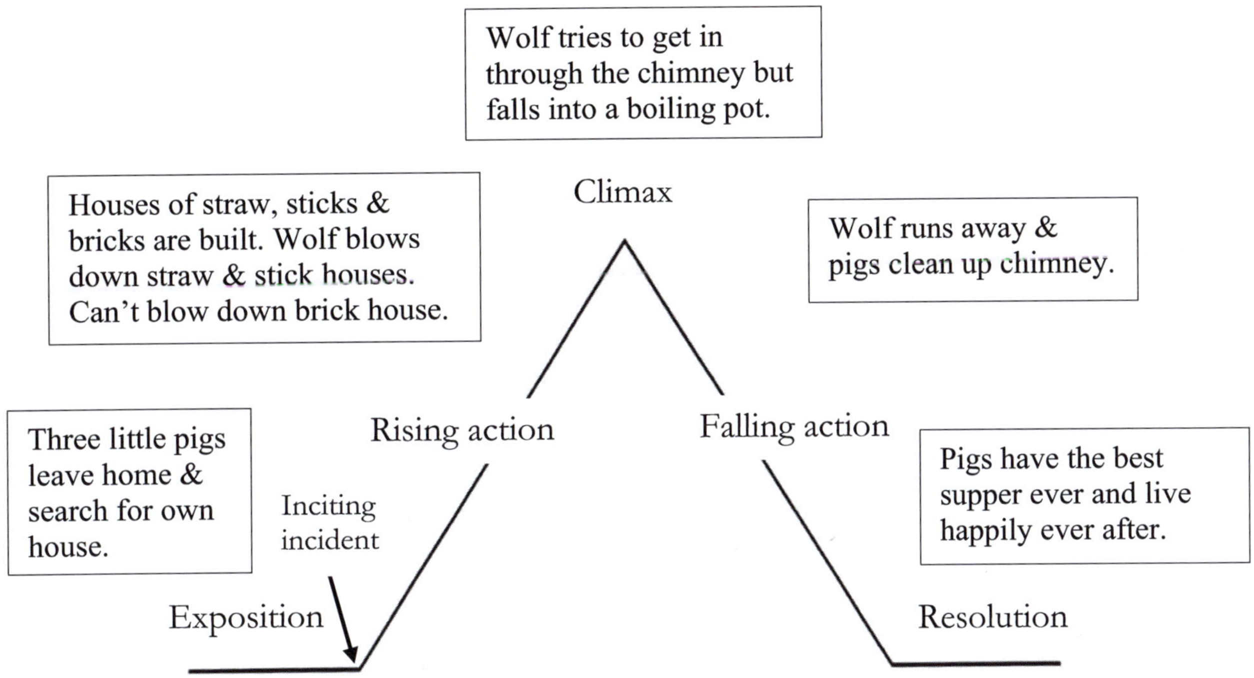

Task 37.

Read the short story in the box below and then see if you can identify the different elements of the plot structure on the next page.

Boastful Brian always thought he was the best at everything. He went around school stating there's no dare he wouldn't do and no challenge he wouldn't take. One day, his friend Jackson dared him into a challenge: "There's a door at the back of the school hall that says, 'DANGER! DO NOT ENTER'. I dare you to open it." At first, Brian didn't want to take the dare, but Jackson wouldn't stop teasing him. Finally, Brian reluctantly agreed to open the door and cautiously moved towards it with outstretched arm. With a sudden pull, Brian flung open the door and immediately fell back in horror. Scores of poisonous snakes escaped and spread across the school, biting everyone in their path. Brian was bitten and poisoned and had to be rushed off to receive emergency medical care. For a number of hours, his life was in the balance. Fortunately, he received treatment just in time. Brian recovered and travelled home to his family. He slept a long sleep. When he woke, he promised never to take a stupid dare again and to change his boastful ways. He had learned his lesson once and for all.

Plot elements: exposition; inciting incident; rising action; climax; falling action; resolution. Write the plot element underneath the correct box.

Scores of poisonous snakes escaped and spread across the school, biting everyone in their path. Brian was bitten and poisoned and had to be rushed off to receive emergency medical care. For a number of hours, his life was in the balance.

____

Finally, Brian reluctantly agreed to open the door and cautiously moved towards it with outstretched arm.

____

Brian recovered and travelled home to his family. He slept a long sleep.

____

Boastful Brian always thought he was the best at everything. He went around school stating there's no dare he wouldn't do and no challenge he wouldn't take.

____

When he woke, he promised never to take a stupid dare again and to change his boastful ways. He had learned his lesson once and for all.

____

One day, his friend Jackson dared him into a challenge. "There's a door at the back of the school hall that says, 'DANGER! DO NOT ENTER'. I dare you to open that door."

____

7 Types of Plot.

There are lots of different types of plot. However, one common approach is to identify seven basic plots. Christopher Booker outlined these in his book "The Seven Basic Plots: Why We Tell Stories."

1. **Overcoming the Monster:**
    - In this plot, the protagonist faces a great evil or formidable antagonist and must overcome it to save themselves or others. Classic examples include Beowulf battling Grendel or St. George slaying the dragon.
2. **Rags to Riches:**
    - The protagonist starts in a humble position and gradually rises to greatness or success. This plot often involves a character's personal or financial improvement. Examples include Cinderella or the classic "rags to riches" tales.
3. **The Quest:**
    - The protagonist embarks on a journey or mission, often with companions, to achieve a significant goal. The quest can be external or internal, and the journey itself is a central element. Examples include "The Lord of the Rings" or "Indiana Jones."
4. **Voyage and Return:**
    - The protagonist enters an unfamiliar or fantastical world, faces challenges, and then returns home transformed. This plot is common in adventure stories and fairy tales. "Alice in Wonderland" is an example of this plot type.
5. **Comedy:**
    - In a comedic plot, misunderstandings, mistaken identities, and confusion lead to a resolution characterized by reconciliation and happiness. Shakespearean comedies, such as "Twelfth Night," often follow this structure.
6. **Tragedy:**
    - Tragedy involves a protagonist with a fatal flaw that leads to their downfall. The plot explores their descent, often culminating in a catastrophic conclusion. Examples include "Hamlet" or "Macbeth" by William Shakespeare.
7. **Rebirth:**
    - The protagonist undergoes a significant inner transformation, experiencing redemption, enlightenment, or a change of heart. This plot type often explores personal growth and renewal. "A Christmas Carol" by Charles Dickens is a classic example.

Not every story neatly fits into one of these categories, but the categories provide a framework for understanding and analysing narrative structures across a wide range of literature and storytelling traditions.

Examples of plot structure. Overcoming the monster.

Title: "Shadows Unveiled".

I. Exposition

A. Setting: A small village surrounded by a dark, ominous forest

B. Protagonist: Mia, a young villager with a mysterious mark on her arm

C. The Monster: The Shadow Beast, a malevolent creature living in the heart of the forest

II. Inciting Event

A. The village is plagued by the Shadow Beast, causing fear and despair

B. Mia finds an ancient prophecy foretelling a chosen one who can defeat Shadow Beast

C. Mia realizes the mark on her arm aligns with the prophecy, making her the chosen one

III. Rising Action

A. Mia sets out on a journey to find a legendary weapon that can kill the Shadow Beast

B. Along the way, Mia encounters challenges that test her courage and determination

C. Mia uncovers the history of the Shadow Beast and its connection to a dark sorcerer who seeks to control it

IV. Climax

A. Mia confronts the Shadow Beast in the heart of the forest

B. The dark sorcerer appears, attempting to manipulate Mia into serving his malevolent plans

C. Mia, driven by inner strength, resists the sorcerer's influence and battles Shadow Beast

V. Falling Action

A. Mia's allies, villagers, and newfound friends join the fight against Shadow Beast

B. The battle intensifies as the prophecy's true power is revealed through Mia's actions

C. The Shadow Beast weakens, and the sorcerer's control over it begins to weaken

VI. Resolution

A. Mia, wielding the legendary weapon, delivers the final blow to the Shadow Beast

B. The darkness retreats, and the village is freed from the grip of fear

C. Mia returns a hero; the mark on her arm fades, marking the end of ancient prophecy

D. The village rebuilds, and Mia's journey becomes a legend, inspiring hope for generations to come.

Title: "Reflections of Destiny".

I. Exposition

A. Setting: A quiet town with an ancient library and a mysterious dusty mirror

B. Protagonist: Alex, a curious and adventurous teenager fascinated by the town's legends

C. Catalyst: Alex finds old journal describing dusty mirror as a portal to a forgotten world

II. Inciting Event

A. Intrigued by the journal, Alex decides to investigate the dusty mirror

B. With a gentle touch, Alex unwittingly activates the mirror, transporting them to a fantastical and otherworldly realm

C. The mirror shatters upon arrival, leaving Alex stranded in the new world

III. Rising Action

A. Alex explores the vibrant, magical land, encountering strange creatures and challenges

B. Along the journey, Alex befriends a guide named Elara, who explains the mirror's significance

C. The duo faces trials that test Alex's courage as they search for ways to repair the mirror

IV. Climax

A. Alex and Elara discover the mirror can only be restored by collecting fragments scattered across the mystical realm

B. The main antagonist, a power-hungry sorcerer, learns of Alex's quest and seeks to harness the mirror's magic for dark purposes

C. Alex and Elara confront the sorcerer in a battle to protect the mirror's fragments

V. Falling Action

A. The mirror's fragments are recovered; the duo returns to the mirror's location in town

B. The sorcerer follows, attempting to seize fragments and control portal for themselves

C. Alex and Elara, with the help of the town's residents, thwart the sorcerer's plans and safeguard the mirror's restoration

VI. Resolution

A. The mirror is rebuilt, and a portal opens, allowing Alex to return to the mystical realm to bid farewell to Elara and the newfound friends

B. Alex returns to the town, forever changed by the adventure, with a newfound appreciation for the extraordinary in the ordinary

C. The dusty mirror, now a symbol of both mystery and connection, remains in the town's lore, waiting for the next curious soul to embark on a voyage and return.

Plot twists

Have you ever read a book where the ending was totally unexpected? That would be an example of what we call a plot twist. A plot twist is a significant change or unexpected development in the storyline of a narrative. The twist often alters the direction of the plot or reveals new information that reshapes the reader's understanding of the story. Plot twists can occur at any point in a narrative, including the beginning, middle or ending. They are designed to surprise, challenge, or provoke emotional responses from the reader and to keep the reader engaged in the story.

Examples of plot twists from children's literature:

"Harry Potter and the Prisoner of Azkaban" by J.K. Rowling: In this episode of the Harry Potter series, the plot twist occurs when it is revealed that Sirius Black, who has been portrayed as a dangerous criminal and the betrayer of Harry's parents, is actually innocent. The true culprit behind the betrayal is revealed to be Peter Pettigrew, who has been hiding in plain sight as Ron's pet rat, Scabbers. This revelation turns the narrative on its head and adds layers of complexity to the characters and their relationships.

"The Lion, the Witch and the Wardrobe" by C.S. Lewis: In C.S. Lewis's classic fantasy novel, the plot twist occurs when it is revealed that Aslan, the noble lion and rightful ruler of Narnia, sacrifices himself to save Edmund, one of the four Pevensie siblings. The twist comes when Aslan returns from the dead, resurrected by the Deep Magic from before the dawn of time. This twist not only adds a profound sense of hope and redemption to the story but also reinforces themes of sacrifice, loyalty, and the triumph of good over evil.

"The Secret Garden" by Frances Hodgson Burnett: In "The Secret Garden," the plot twist occurs when it is revealed that Colin, the sickly and bedridden cousin of the protagonist Mary Lennox, is not actually paralysed as he believes himself to be. With the help of Mary and the healing power of the secret garden, Colin gains strength, confidence, and the ability to walk again. This twist transforms Colin's character arc and adds a sense of renewal and transformation to the narrative.

The Shadow's Secret (plot twist).

Exposition

Introduce the protagonist: 11-year-old Max, an adventurous boy who shares a deep bond with his loyal dog, Buddy.

Set the scene: Max's peaceful town is thrown into chaos when rumours spread of an evil wizard lurking in the nearby woods, spreading darkness and fear.

Inciting Event

Determined to protect his town and uncover the truth about the evil wizard, Max and Buddy set out on a daring adventure into the heart of the woods.

Along the way, they encounter strange creatures and magical obstacles, testing their courage and determination.

Rising Action

As Max and Buddy delve deeper into the woods, they discover clues that lead them to suspect that the evil wizard may be someone they know. Max's suspicions fall on his neighbor, Mr. Jenkins, a reclusive old man rumoured to dabble in dark magic.

Climax/ Plot Twist

Just when Max confronts Mr. Jenkins about his suspicions, Buddy transforms into the evil wizard, revealing himself to be the source of the darkness plaguing the woods. Shocked and betrayed, Max must find a way to stop Buddy and save his town from destruction.

Falling Action

With the help of his friends and the magic of the woods, Max embarks on a quest to uncover the truth about Buddy's transformation and find a way to defeat him.

Along the way, Max learns that Buddy was cursed by an ancient spell and is not truly evil but has been consumed by dark magic.

Resolution

Through love, forgiveness, and the power of their bond, Max is able to break the curse and restore Buddy to his true self.

Max learns valuable lessons about trust, compassion, and the complexities of good and evil, growing into a stronger and wiser individual.

Setting.

Setting is vital for making the scene and story come alive for the reader. If done well, the setting will help to transport the reader into the imaginary world in which your narrative takes place. For effective setting, you want to ask:

- Where does the story happen (see below)
- In what age or period of time (past, present, future)
- What time of year (spring, summer, autumn, winter, midsummer's eve)?
- What time or times of day (dusk, dawn, midnight, afternoon)?
- What is the mood or atmosphere (threatening, joyful, sad, mysterious, scary, exciting, nostalgic)? Does the mood change?
- What is the weather like?

Examples of story locations.

- Desert island
- A room in a house, e.g., the loft.
- Ocean / underwater city
- Underground
- A party
- A dangerous jungle
- Inside a vehicle, e.g., train or plane
- A quiet, country village
- An imaginary world (past, present or future)

A forest
Secret garden or footpath
Mountains
Outer space / another planet
A haunted castle
A dark alleyway
A classroom
A bustling city

Key point: **Make sure your description of the setting is detailed and follows all the principles of effective descriptive writing you learned earlier in this book, including five senses, SHAMPOO and 'show don't tell'.**

Desert island setting.

As the blazing sun hung high in a cloudless azure sky, the desert island lay silent and untouched, except for the rhythmic lapping of gentle waves against the sandy shore. Towering palm trees swayed in the warm breeze, casting long shadows on the pristine white sand. The air was filled with the scent of salt and coconut, carried on the gentle sea breeze. Soaring gracefully overhead, seagulls echoed across the turquoise ocean. In the distance, jagged cliffs rose majestically. Here, on this remote island paradise, time seemed to stand still, offering a sanctuary of solitude amidst the vastness of the sea.

A spooky old loft.

In the dimly lit attic of the old house, shafts of dusty sunlight filtered through cobweb-covered windows, casting eerie patterns on the worn wooden floorboards. Antique trunks and relics were scattered amidst forgotten memories, their surfaces cloaked in a fine layer of age-old dust. The air was heavy with the musty scent of old books and moth-eaten curtains. Ascending into the darkness, a creaky staircase unfolded, its weathered steps groaning softly underfoot, as if bearing the weight of forgotten memories and whispered secrets hidden within the shadows.

The train.

As the train barrelled down the tracks, its rhythmic clatter echoing through the carriage, lonely passengers nestled into their seats, lost in their own world. Outside the window, the landscape blurred into a hazy patchwork of fields, forests, and distant mountains. Inside, the air was humid and thick with anticipation: a palpable energy hummed through the cabin like an electric current.

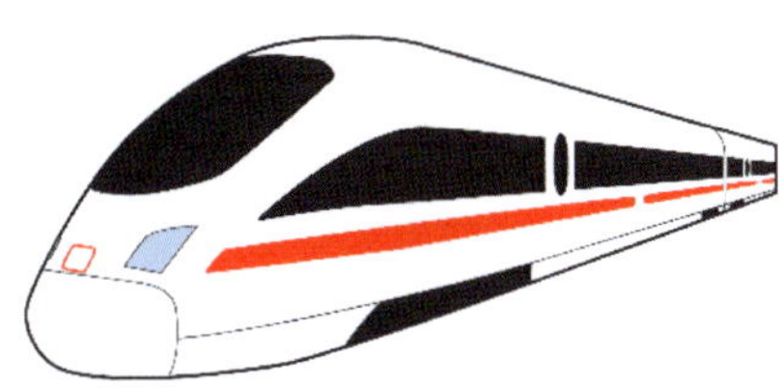

TASK 37. Write a setting for a haunted castle.

What time of year is it?

What can you see?

What time of day is it?

What is the weather like?

Any unusual smells?

What might you find here?

Does the castle or location have a name?

What is the atmosphere? How does the place make you feel?

Write a simile about the place.

What can you hear?

Now write up your setting as a paragraph.

Examples of setting from classical English literature: Charles Dickens.

Look at the example of a brilliant setting description below. This is a description of Smithfield Market in London, in Oliver Twist, by Charles Dickens. On the following page there is an annotated version of the same text to help you better understand its qualities.

> It was market-morning. The ground was covered, nearly ankle-deep, with filth and mire; a thick steam, perpetually rising from the reeking bodies of the cattle, and mingling with the fog, which seemed to rest upon the chimney-tops, hung heavily above. All the pens in the centre of the large area, and as many temporary pens as could be crowded into the vacant space, were filled with sheep; tied up to posts by the gutter side were long lines of beasts and oxen, three or four deep. Countrymen, butchers, drovers, hawkers, boys, thieves, idlers, and vagabonds of every low grade, were mingled together in a mass; the whistling of drovers, the barking of dogs, the bellowing and plunging of oxen, the bleating of sheep, the grunting and squeaking of pigs, the cries of hawkers, the shouts, oaths, and quarrelling on all sides; the ringing of bells and roar of voices, that issued from every public-house; the crowding, pushing, driving, beating, whooping, and yelling; the hideous and discordant din that resounded from every corner of the market; and the unwashed, unshaven, squalid, and dirty figures constantly running to and fro, and bursting in and out of the throng; rendered it a stunning and bewildering scene, which quite confounded the senses.

Annotated example.

It was market-morning. The ground was covered, nearly ankle-deep, with filth and mire; a thick steam, perpetually rising from the reeking bodies of the cattle, and mingling with the fog, which seemed to rest upon the chimney-tops, hung heavily above. All the pens in the centre of the large area, and as many temporary pens as could be crowded into the vacant space, were filled with sheep; tied up to posts by the gutter side were long lines of beasts and oxen, three or four deep. Countrymen, butchers, drovers, hawkers, boys, thieves, idlers, and vagabonds of every low grade, were mingled together in a mass; the whistling of drovers, the barking of dogs, the bellowing and plunging of oxen, the bleating of sheep, the grunting and squeaking of pigs, the cries of hawkers, the shouts, oaths, and quarrelling on all sides; the ringing of bells and roar of voices, that issued from every public-house; the crowding, pushing, driving, beating, whooping, and yelling; the hideous and discordant din that resounded from every corner of the market; and the unwashed, unshaven, squalid, and dirty figures constantly running to and fro, and bursting in and out of the throng; rendered it a stunning and bewildering scene, which quite confounded the senses.

Description of filth and mire: "ankle-deep" immediately gives a sense of the market's unsanitary conditions. This vivid detail sets a gritty & realistic tone, emphasising the harsh reality of the environment.

Atmospheric description: Fog "resting upon the chimney-tops" adds atmosphere, creating a visual image that enhances mood of the scene.

Crowded pens: Repetition of "pens" & emphasis on their being filled convey a sense of overcrowding and chaos. This contributes to the bustling & congested atmosphere of the market.

Sound imagery: Dickens incorporates various sounds that appeal to the sense of hearing. This further immerses the reader in the chaotic & bustling atmosphere of the market. Inclusion of various animal sounds, cries, & human interactions creates a multisensory experience, making the scene more vivid and engaging.

Active Verbs: The use of active verbs like "crowding," "pushing," "driving," "beating," "whooping," & "yelling" conveys a sense of constant motion and energy, contributing to the dynamic and lively nature of the scene.

Descriptive Language: The use of terms like "hideous" and "discordant din" conveys the overwhelming and dissonant nature of the sounds in the market. The description of the figures as "unwashed," "unshaven," "squalid," and "dirty" paints a vivid picture of the physical appearance of the people.

TASK 36.

Annotate the passage below which is a description of Setting from Dickens' A Christmas Carol. Highlight Anything that you think is effective.

Annotate here.

Once upon a time—of all the good days in the year, on Christmas Eve—old Scrooge sat busy in his counting-house. It was cold, bleak, biting weather: foggy too: and he could hear the people in the court outside, go wheezing up and down, beating their hands upon their breasts, and stamping their feet upon the pavement stones to warm them. The city clocks had only just gone three, but it was quite dark already—it had not been light all day—and candles were flaring in the windows of the neighbouring offices, like ruddy smears upon the thick brown air. The fog came pouring in at every chink and keyhole, and was so dense without, that although the court was of the narrowest, the houses opposite were mere phantoms. To see the dingy cloud come drooping down, obscuring everything, one might have thought that Nature lived close by, and was brewing on a large scale.

Characters.

Stop and think for a moment of some of the best and most enjoyable books you have read. Can you remember the main character or characters in those books? I bet you can, even if you have forgotten other details about the book. It is the characters that draw you into the story, move the story forwards and allow you to connect to the fictional world. Can you imagine the Harry Potter series without Harry Potter? We all feel like we know Harry Potter because the author, J. K. Rowling, has done such a great job of making Harry Potter come alive through detailed characterisation. The same could be said for many characters in famous literature, such as Sherlock Holmes, Peter Pan, Cinderella or Jane Eyre.

NOTE: Great books create characters that readers care about. When readers empathise with or relate to characters, they become more involved in the story.

It was said at the beginning of this book that if you want to become an expert at anything, you have to learn from the masters. Likewise, if we want to learn how to write well, we should learn by reading the masters who have gone before us. There are many great writers who are skilled at developing detailed, realistic characters in English literature; however, the one person who stands out above all others is Charles Dickens. Dickens was a master of characterisation. All his main characters are extremely vivid: they are distinctive, detailed and realistic. He often uses humour and metaphor when developing his characters Let's look at two examples. The first is the character of Uriah Heep from the novel David Copperfield. Mr Heep is described as being:

"a red-haired person - a youth of fifteen, as I take it now, but looking much older - whose hair was cropped as close as the closest stubble; who had hardly any eyebrows, and no eyelashes, and eyes of a red-brown, so unsheltered and unshaded, that I remember wondering how he went to sleep. He was high-shouldered and bony; dressed in decent black, with a white wisp of a neckcloth, buttoned up to the throat; and had a long, lank, skeleton hand, which particularly attracted my attention, as he stood at the pony's head, rubbing his chin with it, and looking up at us in the chaise. He had a way of writhing when he wanted to express enthusiasm, which was very ugly."

Annotated example.

"a red-haired person - a youth of fifteen, as I take it now, but looking much older - whose hair was cropped as close as the closest stubble; who had hardly any eyebrows, and no eyelashes, and eyes of a red-brown, so unsheltered and unshaded, that I remember wondering how he went to sleep. He was high-shouldered and bony; dressed in decent black, with a white wisp of a neckcloth; buttoned up to the throat; and had a long, lank, skeleton hand, which particularly attracted my attention, as he stood at the pony's head, rubbing his chin with it, and looking up at us in the chaise. He had a way of writhing when he wanted to express enthusiasm, which was very ugly."

Physical distinctiveness: Dickens creates a physically distinctive image of Uriah Heep. The description of his cropped red hair, lack of eyebrows and eyelashes, and red-brown eyes paints a vivid picture of an unusual and memorable character.

Age discrepancy: The discrepancy between Uriah's appearance (a youth of fifteen) and the impression of looking much older adds an intriguing layer. This discrepancy invites readers to question the reasons behind why he looks so old for his age, suggesting potential hardships or peculiarities in his life.

Unsettling features: The unsettling nature of Uriah's features, such as his red-brown eyes without shelter or shade, contributes to a sense of discomfort and adds an eerie quality to the character.

Detailed clothing: The detailed description of Uriah's clothing, including the decent black clothing and the white neckcloth buttoned up to the throat, contributes to the overall characterisation. His careful dressing hints at a desire to present himself as respectable despite his peculiarities.

Distinctive physical movements: The mention of Uriah's long, lank, skeleton hand and his way of writhing to express enthusiasm adds more layers to his characterisation. These physical details and movements become symbolic of his nature, making him stand out as a unique and memorable character.

Descriptive language: Dickens's choice of descriptive language, such as "high-shouldered and bony," paints a clear and interesting picture. The language is specific and imaginative, allowing readers to easily visualise Uriah Heep.

Setting the tone: The description sets the tone for Uriah Heep's character, creating a sense of unease and curiosity. Readers are likely to be intrigued by the peculiarities of this character, setting the stage for further exploration of his role in the narrative.

Personality insights: While the description focuses on Uriah Heep's physical attributes, it also offers little hints about his character. The use of words like "ugly" in describing his way of writhing suggests a certain unpleasantness or dishonesty in his character.

TASK 34.

Read this description of Ebeneezer Scrooge from Charles Dickens' novella A Christmas Carol. Go through it carefully and annotate it with the help of the boxes.

"Oh! But he was a tight-fisted hand at the grindstone, Scrooge! a squeezing, wrenching, grasping, scraping, clutching, covetous, old sinner! Hard and sharp as flint, from which no steel had ever struck out generous fire; secret, and self-contained, and solitary as an oyster. The cold within him froze his old features, nipped his pointed nose, shrivelled his cheek, stiffened his gait; made his eyes red, his thin lips blue; and spoke out shrewdly in his grating voice. A frosty rime was on his head, and on his eyebrows, and his wiry chin. He carried his own low temperature always about with him; he iced his office in the dog-days; and didn't thaw it one degree at Christmas."

Imagery:

Figurative language (metaphors / similes):

Alliteration & repetition:

Character traits:

Physical reflection of his personality:

Any other things of note:

Principles of effective characterisation.

Characterisation:

- Physical Traits: Describe the appearance of your characters. Include details such as age, height, weight, hair color, and any distinctive features.
- Personality: Develop personalities that are unique and interesting. Consider strengths, weaknesses, fears, and desires. How do they react to different situations?

Background:

- Create a backstory for your characters explaining their past experiences, upbringing, and significant life events.

Character Arc:

- Characters can either be **static** or **dynamic**. Dynamic characters change through the story. Static characters do not change. Most protagonists are dynamic characters. For example, Scrooge is a dynamic character: he starts off mean and stingy and ends up kind and generous after going through some life-changing experiences.
- Motivations: Clearly define what your characters want and what drives them. Understanding motivations helps shape their decisions and actions in the story.

Roles in the Story:

- Protagonist: The main character whom readers follow and root for. The protagonist often faces challenges and undergoes significant growth.
- Antagonist: The character or force that opposes the protagonist, creating conflict. Antagonists can be individuals, groups, or even internal struggles.
- Supporting Characters: These characters contribute to the overall narrative, aiding or hindering the protagonist. They add depth and complexity to the story.

Conflict and Relationships:

- Characters often come into conflict with each other, either internally or externally. These conflicts drive the plot and reveal more about the characters.
- Explore relationships between characters. Whether familial, friendly, romantic, or adversarial, relationships add depth and emotion to the story.

TASK 35.

Create an imaginary character by completing the boxes. See the example first.

Character development

Character name: ____________________

What does the character look

Average height, athletic build, 27 years old, youthful, olive skin, freckles, chestnut hair, shoulder length, loose braid, hazel eyes, upright posture

What is the character wearing?

Worn-in hiking boots, loose-fitting khaki trousers, black hoodie, belt with eagle, scarlet leather, fingerless gloves, leather bracelet, gold neckless with hammer

At the beginning my character is: Reclusive & solitary, unwilling to trust others; mean; miserable, melancholic; rude, cold-hearted.

At the end my character is / has: compassionate, open-hearted; has a newfound sense of purpose. Sociable & friendly; generous and caring.

Why did the character change? Unexpected challenges and experiences. Realises the importance of kindness and charity.

Task 35.

Create an imaginary character by completing the boxes below.

Character development

What does the character look

What is the character wearing?

Characters can either be **static** or **dynamic**. Dynamic characters change through the story. Static characters do not change through the story. Most protagonists are dynamic characters. For example, Scrooge is a dynamic character: he starts off mean and stingy and ends up kind and generous after going through some life-changing experiences. Complete the boxes below. **If your character is static, you only need to complete the first box.** Look at all the character adjectives on the next page for inspiration.

At the beginning my character is:	At the end my character is / has:	How did the character change?

Positive characteristics.

admirable adventurous affable affectionate agreeable altruistic amiable articulate assertive assiduous assured astute benevolent bold brainy brave calm candid cautious charismatic charming cheerful collegial comical compassionate confident congenial conscientious considerate courageous curious courteous decisive devoted diligent diplomatic discerning distinguished droll earnest eclectic elegant eloquent eminent enchanting energetic enthusiastic erudite faithful formidable frugal funny gallant generous genial gentle gifted glamorous graceful gracious gregarious hardy honourable hospitable humble humorous impartial impeccable indolent indomitable industrious ingenious inquisitive intrepid jocular jolly jovial judicious liberal loyal magnanimous magnificent merciful methodical meticulous mischievous moderate modern modest noble optimistic perceptive philanthropic philosophical pious placid pragmatic precocious principled prophetic prudent punctual rational reasonable reflective resilient resourceful sagacious scrupulous self-disciplined self-effacing shrewd sincere sober sociable sophisticated steadfast stoic stout tenacious thrifty tolerant tough unpretentious venerable vivacious witty zany

Negative characteristics.

aggressive aloof annoying antagonistic arrogant artful authoritarian awkward baleful bellicose belligerent boastful boisterous callous cantankerous capricious clumsy coarse conceited coy crass crazy curt daring deceptive depraved despotic devious disinterested docile dogmatic dour dull duplicitous egotistical erratic evil facile fastidious fatuous feeble fickle flippant foolhardy foolish frail frivolous glib gluttonous greedy grumpy gullible haughty heartless heedless horrible idle ignominious ignorant impetuous imperious imprudent impudent impulsive inept infamous insolent insular irascible irrational irreverent lazy Machiavellian malevolent malicious mediocre menacing misanthropic miserly monotonous morbid naïve nasty nonchalant notorious nutty obdurate obnoxious obsequious obsessive obstinate obstreperous obtuse odd odious officious ostentatious pathetic patronising pedantic pessimistic petty petulant pompous pretentious prodigal profligate pugnacious querulous recalcitrant reclusive reprehensible rowdy ruthless sanctimonious sarcastic scary scurrilous selfish self-righteous servile silly slothful slovenly sly spendthrift spiteful stern stingy stubborn submissive subservient supercilious superficial surly sycophantic tardy terse testy thoughtless timid trite unscrupulous vain vapid vindictive volatile vulgar weird wicked zealous

Neutral or can be both negative and positive characteristics.

ascetic audacious blunt brazen contemporary conventional cunning decadent diffident dispassionate eccentric elusive enigmatic extrovert fierce flamboyant garrulous grandiose introspective introvert laconic loquacious meek melancholic mercurial mysterious obedient obscure outgoing peculiar pensive reverent rueful sceptical taciturn unforgiving verbose vociferous voracious whimsical

Narrative tension.

In order to make your story interesting and exciting, you need to introduce tension. There are some simple and effective ways to do this.

Foreshadowing: Drop hints or clues in the story about future events, building anticipation and unease. For example, the protagonist notices a mysterious figure lurking in the shadows near the crime scene. This hint suggests that there may be more to the story than meets the eye, building anticipation and unease in the reader as they wonder about the figure's identity and motives.

As Sarah walked home from work, she couldn't shake the feeling that someone was following her, their shadowy presence lurking just beyond her peripheral vision.

Conflict: Introduce obstacles, challenges, or conflicts that the characters must overcome. This could be external conflict (e.g., a villain, natural disaster) or internal conflict (e.g., moral dilemmas, inner struggles).

The dragon roared, its fiery breath scorching the earth as it clashed with the brave knight, their swords clanging in a fierce battle for dominance.

Time pressure: Create a sense of urgency by imposing deadlines or time limits on the characters' actions, raising the stakes and increasing tension as the clock ticks down.

With only minutes left before the bomb detonated, Detective Smith raced against the clock, his heart pounding in his chest as he frantically searched for the hidden explosives.

Secrets and revelations: Introduce secrets, mysteries, or hidden agendas that characters keep from each other or the reader, gradually revealing them over time to heighten suspense and intrigue.

With each new diary entry she uncovered, Elizabeth's heart sank as she unearthed the dark family secrets that had been hidden for generations.

Suspenseful pacing: Control the pacing of the story by alternating between moments of calm and tension, using shorter sentences and paragraphs, cliffhangers, and unexpected plot twists to keep the reader engaged.

With every step down the dark hallway, Sarah's heart pounded louder in her ears. The suspense became unbearable as she neared the room where the killer lay in wait. Her breathing quickened. She began to sweat.

High stakes: Raise the stakes by putting characters in situations where the potential consequences of failure are significant, such as risking their lives, losing loved ones, or facing moral dilemmas.

As the timer ticked down to the final seconds, he realised that defusing the bomb was his only chance to save the hostages trapped in the building.

Uncertainty and ambiguity: Leave certain elements of the story open to interpretation or unresolved, allowing readers to speculate and wonder about the outcome, creating tension as they seek answers.

As he reached for the door handle, he couldn't shake the feeling that something was not right, but he couldn't quite put his finger on it.

Unexpected events: Unexpected events add tension by disrupting the expected flow of the narrative and introducing uncertainty. They catch the characters and the reader off guard, creating a sense of unease and anticipation about what might happen next.

As she stepped into the dimly lit hallway, she suddenly heard the sound of shattering glass coming from the room ahead, sending a jolt of fear coursing through her veins.

Just as Lian thought he had escaped the pursuing enemy, a sudden explosion rocked the ground beneath his feet, sending debris flying in all directions and plunging them into a new, more perilous situation.

TASK 35.

Write your own sentences for the following, generating tension where possible.

Foreshadowing:

Time pressure:

Unexpected events:

Conflict:

Sample.

One previous 11+ exam paper contained the following question. *Write a story with the starting line: 'This was a lofty chamber, lined and littered with countless bottles.'* Here is a model answer to that question and annotated version on the following page.

This was a lofty chamber, lined and littered with countless bottles; the room stretched upward, to the ceiling like a book with too many pages. Light streamed in through dust-coated windows, revealing a jumble of shelves adorned with bottles of all sizes and colours.

At the heart of this curious place stood Professor Norbert Peacock – a man with clumps of messy white hair and round spectacles perched on the edge of his nose. His fingers danced over the labels of the bottles, as he searched desperately for the potion that would save humanity from a deadly disease.

"I know the solution lies somewhere within these bottles" he cried in desperation; "If only I knew which one!"

One bottle, thin and corked, held a midnight-blue liquid that shimmered like a starlit sky. Another, short and fat, contained a potion that sparkled with silver lava. The chamber seemed to hum with the whispers of ancient knowledge contained within the bottles while an aroma combining sweet pine and bitter sulphur spread through the room.

Like two big pearls, the professor's eyes scanned the room as if trying to solve the mystery of the universe. Pacing up and down, he knew that if he got this wrong, it could end in disaster. Sweat began to form on his brow while the walls seemed to glare with nervousness.

Suddenly, the professor paused before a dusty book, its leather cover worn with time. Its pages held the key to a secret potion that Professor Peacock had been seeking for years. "Aha!" the professor exclaimed. He felt a burst of determination as his fingers traced the diagrams and formulas in the antique book.

Dipping below the horizon outside the window, the sun cast a warm embrace over his room, as the air seemed to hold its breath expectantly, waiting for the results of the professor's efforts.

With a triumphant smile, he seized a bottle – its contents a vibrant gold potion bubbling and shimmering in the fading daylight. Uncorking it with a gasp, the professor's eyes sparkled with the satisfaction of a puzzle finally solved.

In that lofty chamber, lined and littered with countless bottles, Professor Norbert Peacock had worked his magic, finding a potion that would save the world.

Yellow: language. techniques & imagery
Green: punctuation & dialogue
Pink: structure & narrative tension

The phrase "lofty chamber" establishes a sense of height and elegance. Repeated "l" creates alliteration.

"Room stretched upward" Personification of the room, giving it human-like qualities.

Semi-colon - variety of punctuation & sentence forms.

Simile suggests room full of information.

This was a lofty chamber, lined and littered with countless bottles; the room stretched upward, to the ceiling like a book with too many pages. Light streamed in through dust-coated windows, revealing a jumble of shelves adorned with bottles of all sizes and colours.

"streamed" creates visual imagery; "adorned" = interesting verb.

Opener: preposition

Descriptive details of Prof. Peacock create distinctive + vivid character which is more engaging.

Urgent search for potion (inciting incident) adds tension + moves plot forward.

At the heart of this curious place stood Professor Norbert Peacock – a man with clumps of messy white hair and round spectacles perched on the edge of his nose. His fingers danced over the labels of the bottles, as he searched desperately for the potion that would save humanity from a deadly disease.

Personification

Speech adds realism to character + story; varied punctuation used.

"I know the solution lies somewhere within these bottles", he cried in desperation; "If only I knew which one!"

Visual imagery created by interesting description and simile.

Sound imagery, sibilance + personification add to mystery + atmosphere.

Smell imagery helps to engage reader and adds realism.

One bottle, thin and corked, held a midnight-blue liquid that shimmered like a starlit sky. Another, short and fat, contained a potion that sparkled with silver lava. The chamber seemed to hum with the whispers of ancient knowledge contained within the bottles while an aroma combining sweet pine and bitter sulphur spread through the room.

Complex sentence.

Simile + metaphor create vivid imagery.

High stakes tension created.

Opener: verb.

Personification of walls adds emotion + boosts sense of expectation.

Like two big pearls, the professor's eyes scanned the room as if trying to solve the mystery of the universe. Pacing up and down, he knew that if he got this wrong, it could end in disaster. Sweat began to form on his brow while the walls seemed to glare with nervousness...

Ellipses indicates nervous moment / cliff hanger.

Zooms in to Prof. Peacock's reactions; helps reader to engage with character and looming disaster boosts tension.

Openers: adverb.

Texture appeals to sense of touch.

Secrecy creates tension. "Aha!" indicates the start of the narrative climax.

Suddenly, the professor paused before a dusty book, its leather cover worn with time. Its pages held the key to a secret potion that Professor Peacock had been seeking for years. "Aha!" the professor exclaimed; he felt a burst of determination as his fingers traced the diagrams and formulas in the antique book.

Openers: verb.

Personification of the sun makes it more relatable for the reader.

Personification of the air reinforces anticipation.

Dipping below the horizon outside the window, the sun cast a warm embrace over his room, as the air seemed to hold its breath expectantly, waiting for the results of the professor's efforts.

Openers: preposition.

Openers: participial phrase.

Sibilance reinforces excitement.

With a triumphant smile, he seized a bottle – its contents a vibrant gold potion, bubbling and shimmering in the fading daylight. Uncorking it with a gasp, the professor's eyes sparkled with the satisfaction of a puzzle finally solved.

Ending echoes beginning creating harmonious narrative structure.

Resolution provides a satisfying ending.

In that lofty chamber, lined and littered with countless bottles, Professor Norbert Peacock had worked his magic, finding a potion that would save the world.

What good features does this story have?

- Varied use of sentence forms
- Varied openers
- Varied use of punctuation
- Variety of techniques (personification, alliteration, similes, metaphor etc.)
- Interesting, descriptive verbs and adjectives
- Quirky character and vivid setting details using five senses and imagery
- Narrative tension

Remember the plot and the features and try your own version of this story.

Narrative perspective.

Narrative perspective is the point of view from which a story is told. It determines who is narrating the story and how much insight the reader has into the thoughts, feelings, and experiences of the characters. There are different narrative perspectives, each offering a unique view through which the story is presented. Here are some examples:

First-Person Perspective: In first-person perspective, the story is narrated by a character within the story, using "I" or "we" pronouns. This perspective provides a direct view into the narrator's thoughts, emotions, and experiences, but it may be limited to what the narrator knows or perceives. Example: "I walked down the dimly lit street, my heart pounding with anticipation."

Third-Person Limited Perspective: In third-person limited perspective, the story is narrated by an external narrator who focuses on the thoughts and experiences of one character, using "he," "she," or "they" pronouns. This perspective allows for some insight into the character's inner world, but it remains limited to that character's perspective. The narrator is not part of the story. Example: "Sarah watched the storm clouds gather on the horizon, feeling a sense of unease creep over her."

Third-Person Omniscient Perspective: In this perspective, the story is narrated by an all-knowing external narrator who has insight into the thoughts, feelings, and experiences of multiple characters. This perspective offers a broader view of the story world and allows the narrator to move freely between different characters' perspectives. Example: "As John approached the door, he hesitated, unsure if he should knock. Meanwhile, inside the house, Mary paced back and forth, her mind racing with worry."

Second-Person Perspective: In second-person perspective, the story is narrated directly to the reader, using "you" pronouns. This perspective can create a sense of immediacy and involvement, as if the reader is experiencing the events of the story firsthand. Example: "You stand at the edge of the cliff, the wind whipping through your hair as you gaze out at the endless expanse of the ocean below." *The Night Circus*, by Erin Morgenstern, is an example of a novel written in second person.

Narrative template – plan your story

Title of your story

Exposition – introduce your characters, setting and the plot

Rising action – build your plot with different events

Climax – what is the most dramatic and exciting part?

Resolution - how does your story end?

CHECK YOUR WORK

Your writing is NEVER finished until you have checked it. Checking your work is the platinum rule of all good writing. Over 25 years of teaching and marking, I have unfortunately seen many students fail tests because of silly, simple mistakes that they would have picked up if they had checked their work. ALWAYS make sure you check your work. Below is a checklist you should use every time you produce a piece of writing. Don't forget!!

1. Have I used at least 3 SHAMPOOs? ☐

2. Have I used at least 3 of the 5 senses? ☐

3. Have I used strong, descriptive nouns, verbs and adjectives? ☐

3. Have I used varied sentence forms (simple, compound, complex)? ☐

4. Have I used varied punctuation? ☐

5. Are my tenses consistent? ☐

6. Are there any spelling or grammar mistakes? ☐

Add your own checkpoints as you wish.

Recommended reading list for age 9-12.

"The Starlight Stables Gang" by Esme Higgs, Jo Cotterill & Hannah George (2023)

"Rockstar Detectives: Murder at the Movies" by Adam Hills & Luna Valentine (2023)

"The First Shadowdragon" by Lee Newbury & Laura Catalán (2023)

"The Sun and the Star" by Rick Riordan & Mark Oshiro (2023)

"Stolen History" by Sathnam Sanghera (2023)

"Momo Arashima Steals the Sword of the Wind" by Misa Sugiura (2023)

"The Ministry of Unladylike Activity" by Robin Stevens (2022)

"The Attack of the Robot Librarians" by Sam Copeland & Jenny Pearson (2023)

"Lil' Muffin Drops the Mic" by Romesh Ranganathan & James Lancett (2023)

"Brother Wulf: Wulf's War" by Joseph Delaney (2023)

"The Good Turn" by Sharna Jackson (2022)

"The Double Trouble Society" by Carrie Hope Fletcher & Davide Ortu (2022)

"Wilder than Midnight" by Cerrie Burnell (2022)

"Charlotte's Web" by E. B. White (1952)

"Frankie Best Hates Quests" by Chris Smith & Kenneth Anderson (2022)

"The Catastrophic Friendship Fails of Lottie Brooks" by Katie Kirby (2022)

"Goodnight Mister Tom" by Michelle Magorian (1981)

"Kay's Marvellous Medicine" by Adam Kay & Henry Paker (2021)

"Diary of a Wimpy Kid" by Jeff Kinney (2023)

"Wonder" by R. J. Palacio (2012)

"Matilda" by Roald Dahl (1988)

"Harry Potter and the Sorcerer's Stone" by J.K. Rowling (1997)

"The Secret Garden" by Frances Hodgson Burnett (1911)

"Where the Red Fern Grows" by Wilson Rawls (1961)

"The Boxcar Children" by Gertrude Chandler Warner (1924)

"Anne of Green Gables" by L.M. Montgomery (1908)

"The Chronicles of Narnia: The Lion, the Witch and the Wardrobe" by C.S. Lewis (1950)

"Charlie and the Chocolate Factory" by Roald Dahl (1964)

"The Secret of the Old Clock" (Nancy Drew Mystery Stories) by Carolyn Keene (1930)

"Holes" by Louis Sachar (1998)

"Island of the Blue Dolphins" by Scott O'Dell (1960)

"Number the Stars" by Lois Lowry (1989)

"The BFG" by Roald Dahl (1982)

"The Indian in the Cupboard" by Lynne Reid Banks (1980)

"Stuart Little" by E.B. White (1945)

"A Wrinkle in Time" by Madeleine L'Engle (1962)

"The Wind in the Willows" by Kenneth Grahame (1908)

"The Adventures of Tintin" series by Hergé (1929 onwards)

"The Magic Tree House" series by Mary Pope Osborne (1992 onwards)

"James and the Giant Peach" by Roald Dahl (1961)

"Little House on the Prairie" by Laura Ingalls Wilder (1935)

"The Mysterious Benedict Society" by Trenton Lee Stewart (2007)

"How to Train Your Dragon" series by Cressida Cowell (2003 onwards)

"Bridge to Terabithia" by Katherine Paterson (1977)

"The One and Only Ivan" by Katherine Applegate (2012)

"The Giver" by Lois Lowry (1993)

"The Little Prince" by Antoine de Saint-Exupéry (1943)

"The Neverending Story" by Michael Ende (1979)

"The Witches" by Roald Dahl (1983)

"The Percy Jackson & the Olympians" series by Rick Riordan (2005 onwards)

"The Secret Series" by Enid Blyton (1929 onwards)

"The Berenstain Bears" series by Stan and Jan Berenstain (1962 onwards)

"The 39 Clues" series by various authors (2008 onwards)

"The Miraculous Journey of Edward Tulane" by Kate DiCamillo (2006)

"The Enchanted Wood" (The Faraway Tree series) by Enid Blyton (1939)

"The Secret Seven" series by Enid Blyton (1949 onwards)

"The Wonderful Wizard of Oz" by L. Frank Baum (1900)

"The Cricket in Times Square" by George Selden (1960)

"The Mysterious Disappearance of Leon (I Mean Noel)" by Ellen Raskin (1971)

"The Great Brain" series by John D. Fitzgerald (1967 onwards)

"Harriet the Spy" by Louise Fitzhugh (1964)

“Impossible Creatures” by Katherine Rundell (2023)

“Peanut Jones and the Illustrated City” by Rob Biddulph. 2021.

“Malamander (An Eerie-on-Sea Mystery)” by Thomas Taylor (2019)

“The Call of the Wild” by Jack London (2011)

“The Hound of the Baskervilles” by Arthur Conan Doyle (2011)

“Alice’s Adventures in Wonderland” by Lewis Carroll (1895)

Answers.

Task 1. Suggested answers:
Sight: sand, beach, coast, water, waves, blue, azure, cyan, sapphire, sun, clouds, trees, palms, hut, swimming pools, flowers, boats, people, birds.
Sound: whispering breeze, rustling leaves, boats, waves, splashing water, sea, birds, seagulls, voices, music,
Smell: sea, sea salt, seaweed, fresh air, coffee, barbecue, sweets, pines, trees, flowers of all kinds
Touch: breeze, sand, water, warmth of sun, grass

Task 2. Page 6.
"The Ascent" is a narrative. "The Mountainside" is a description.

Task 3. Page 8. Identify nouns, verbs, adjectives and adverbs. Sort them into correct boxes below.

Nouns elegance, tree, lighthouse, meadow, pain, gallery, ocean, sunset, chess, practice	Verbs Observe, compose, chuckle, float, persuade, saunter, practise, amble, gallop, wither,

Adjectives Ginormous, majestic, incredible, fast, elegant, calm, graceful, peculiar, complicated, jubilant	Adverbs Sometimes, cautiously, well, speedily, never, incredibly, suddenly, intensely, often, meticulously, fast

Note: "fast" can be both an adjective and an adverb.

Task 4. Page 10.

It <u>was</u> 5pm. The rain <u>was</u> heavy. It <u>fell</u> continuously, while Jack <u>walked</u> home from work. As soon as he <u>arrived</u> home, he <u>opened</u> the door and <u>went</u> inside. He <u>took</u> off his coat, <u>sat</u> down in the chair and <u>slept</u>.

Task 5. Page 10. Suggested answer.

It was 5pm. The sun **dazzled** down on the valley. Its rays of heat **radiated** on Jack's face. The gentle breeze **whispered** through the trees. The trees **rocked** from side to side. High above, clouds **drifted** across the sky. Birds **soared** high into the clouds. Mountains **stood** surrounding the town. In the garden, children were **slurping** ice cream and dogs were **leaping** in the air.

Task 6. Page 11. Find more descriptive verbs to replace the boring verbs. Suggested answers.

The dog walked along the street.
(The dog sauntered...)
The girl drank her cola quickly.
(The girl gulped...)
The cow chewed the grass.
(The cow munched...)
Jenny walked in the park.
(Jenny strolled...)
The wind blew against the trees.
(The wind crashed...)

The train moved quickly down the track.
(The train rocketed...)
The mouse ate the cheese.
(The mouse nibbled...)
I love chocolate ice cream.
(I adore...)
Rain hit against the roof.
(Rain smashed...)
Leaves moved in the breeze.
(Leaves rocked...)

Task 7. Page 13. Underline the noun.

<u>Tom</u> unhooked the <u>latch</u> on the <u>door</u> and went into the <u>garden</u>. He saw beautiful <u>flowers</u> and some <u>water</u>. <u>Birds</u> circled above and a <u>dog</u> lay in the <u>grass</u>. There were <u>people</u> sitting on a <u>piece of material</u>, eating <u>food</u>. Tall <u>trees</u> cast long <u>shadows</u> across the <u>street</u>. There was a <u>path</u> that ran through the <u>garden</u>. He followed the <u>path</u> and came to a <u>building</u>. Outside the <u>building</u> there was a parked <u>car</u> and two <u>people</u> playing a <u>game</u>. Another <u>person</u> was riding an <u>animal</u>.

Task 7. Re-write the passage using more interesting nouns. Suggested answer.

Tom unhooked the latch on the <u>oak</u> door and went into the garden. He saw beautiful <u>daisies</u> and <u>daffodils</u> and a <u>waterfall</u>. <u>Sparrows</u> circled above and a <u>terrier</u> lay in the meadow. There were <u>teenagers</u> sitting on a <u>woollen picnic mat</u>, eating <u>pizza</u>. Tall <u>birch trees</u> cast long shadows across the street. There was a <u>stone path</u> that ran through the garden. Tom followed the path and came to a large <u>palace</u>. Outside the <u>palace</u> there was a parked <u>limousine</u> and two <u>boys</u> playing <u>basketball</u>. A <u>man</u> was riding a <u>horse</u>.

Task 8. Page 14. Re-write the sentences below using more descriptive or more concise nouns.

1. The <u>teenager</u> was playing a <u>guitar</u>.
2. My <u>son</u> likes to play <u>football</u>.
3. There was a <u>beetle</u> crawling across the <u>table</u>.
4. The <u>oil</u> began to burn.
5. We travelled across the ocean in a <u>hovercraft</u>.
6. The <u>president</u> stepped inside a <u>limousine</u>.
7. Mike turned the corner and saw a large <u>castle</u>.
8. In the army soldiers use <u>camouflage.</u>
9. The garden was full of <u>conifers / oaks / beech.</u>

Task 9. Page 16. Rewrite the passage using more descriptive nouns and adjectives.

It was a stunning day. The golden sun was shining and the sapphire sky was spectacular. The cottage was massive. It had a scarlet oak door and an iron frame. It had an inviting garden with exquisite roses. Huge emerald beech trees stretched upwards to touch the delicious pearl-white clouds. Within its walls, an adorable living room featured a charming oak bookshelf. The family enjoyed a hearty dinner at the impressive dining table, surrounded by warmth and love.

Underline the adjective.

It was a fine day. The yellow sun was shining and the blue sky was really amazing. The house was big. It had a red, wooden door and a metal frame. It had a nice garden with nice flowers. Big, green trees stretched upwards to touch the lovely white clouds. Within its walls, a beautiful living room featured a beautiful, wooden bookshelf. The family enjoyed a good dinner at the nice dining table, surrounded by warmth and love.

Rewrite the passage with descriptive adjectives. Suggested answer.

It was a glorious day. The golden sun shone through the sparkling, sapphire sky. A grandiose house stood proud with a chestnut, mahogany door and a steel frame. It had an exquisite garden adorned with vibrant blossoms. Majestic, emerald elms reached upwards to fluffy, silverish clouds. Within the stone walls, a stunning living room featured a charming, pine bookshelf. The close-knit family devoured a scrumptious dinner at the grand dining table, surrounded by warmth and love.

Task 10. Page 18. Write 10 descriptive sentences using unusual colours. Page 18

1. (sky) Shimmering through the clouds, the sapphire sky beckoned the seagulls.
2. (ocean) The azure ocean lapped against the shore.
3. (hair) Chestnut locks of hair were flowing over the girl's shoulders.
4. (sunshine) Radiating golden sunshine embraced the land.
5. (forest) A forest of emerald and pine lay in front of me.
6. Crimson-coloured petals led the way through the garden path.
7. Ivory clouds drifted steadily across the cobalt sky.
8. Forest-green leaves huddled around caramel-coloured branches.

Quick knowledge check. Page 20.

A redundant adverb is one that adds no meaning to the sentence.
An example of a bland adverb is "really" or "very". Credit other reasonable answers.
An example of a weak verb is "walk" or "said". Credit other reasonable answers.
Examples of strong verbs include "trudged" or "exclaimed".
Other words for red include "crimson", "scarlet", "ruby", "rose".

Other words for blue include “cobalt”, “sapphire”, “azure”.

Task 11. Page 21. Highlight adjectives and adverbs.

It was 12am midnight. Kingsley was on his final mission. The cold, icy air penetrated his skin sharply. The bright moon, which was shining intensely through the clouds, hung in the sky like a precious, pure pearl; its glowing light spread thoroughly across the dark blue sky. Kingsley looked straight ahead and could just about see a dark silhouette forming vaguely on the horizon. As he moved steadily closer, the vague silhouette turned gradually into the definite, clear contours of a house standing eerily over the valley. At either side of the house there were different types of extremely tall, green trees, standing proudly and protectively like night watchmen. The house seemed to be watching him intently. Up above, a black raven hovered suspiciously over the house. The total, sinister silence was brazenly broken only by the distant, faraway sounds of wolves howling menacingly. Kingsley, who was now feeling really scared, walked forward cautiously.

Task 12. Re-write and improve the passage.

At midnight, Kingsley embarked on his final mission, braving the penetrating icy air. The moon, a brilliant pearl, sparkled through the clouds, casting its glow across the midnight sky. Ahead, a dark silhouette gradually transformed into a clear house standing eerily over the valley. Tall trees flanked the house like vigilant night watchmen. Above, a jet-black raven hovered ominously. A sinister silence permeated, interrupted only by distant wolf howls. Kingsley, increasingly frightened, inched forward.

Quick Check. True or False. Page 24.

The subject comes before the predicate.	T
The subject modifies the noun.	F
The predicate tells us something about the noun.	T
The subject is the thing that the sentence is about.	T

Task 13. Page 26.

1. When I need to finish my homework, I stay up late. D
2. I don’t like sprouts. I
3. Before I go out, I must take a shower. D
4. I want to travel the world and taste different types of cuisine. I
5. I will deal with that problem after I return from work. D
6. The Nile is the longest river in the world. I
7. It rains a lot in London though it doesn’t snow too often. D
8. It rained last night, but it wasn’t very heavy. I

9. Too many cooks spoil the broth. I
10. Never let a fool kiss you, or a kiss fool you. I
11. I'll join you as long as you don't stay too late. D
12. Although I'm not the biggest fan of Star Wars, I went to see it anyway. D
13. If I win the lottery, I'll share half with you. D
14. The best things in life are free. I
15. The best things in life are free, and I like free stuff. I

Task 14. Page 29. Identify compound, complex and simple sentences.

1. She walked to the park. **Simple**.
2. While she was walking to the park, she spotted a colourful butterfly. **Complex**.
3. The beautiful sun was shining brightly. **Simple**.
4. Although the sun was shining brightly, it felt chilly in the breeze. **Complex**.
5. He decided to go for a swim, but he realised he forgot his swimsuit. **Compound**.
6. The cat meowed loudly. **Simple**.
7. When the cat meowed loudly, it was asking for attention. **Complex**.
8. They baked cookies for the school fundraiser. **Simple**.
9. They baked cookies for school, and they sold them all in a few hours. **Compound**.
10. She walked to the park, and her friends joined her. **Compound**.
11. The sun was rising but it was still cold. **Compound**.
12. I like going to Spain because it's warm there. **Complex**.
13. The quick, brown fox jumped over the lazy cat. **Simple**.
14. What is it like to grow up on a farm? **Simple**.
15. I won't go out unless it stops raining. **Complex**.

Task 15. Page 33. Are these sentences correct? If not, write the correct version below.

1. Incorrect. Correct version: Jenny went to the store to buy milk, cheese, chicken, beans and meat.
2. Incorrect. Correct version: Frequently, my mom cleans my bedroom.
3. Incorrect. Correct version: I can't stand the smell of fish, but I love the smell of lemon.
4. Incorrect. Correct version: Jimmy's car, which he bought last year, is in need of repair.
5. Incorrect. Correct version: My favourite colour is black, not white. (optional comma after black).
6. Incorrect. Correct version: My sister loves to play soccer, but she hates basketball.
7. Incorrect. Correct version: The small, fluffy, adorable puppy played in the sunny garden.
8. Incorrect. Correct version: "I need help", she screamed.
9. Incorrect. Correct version: While I was walking, the dog was barking.
10. Incorrect. Correct version: All of a sudden, Jim jumped out of the water.

Task 16. Page 36. Are the following sentences correct? If not, write the correct version below.

1. Incorrect. Correct version: Because of the heavy snow this evening, we won't be going to work tomorrow.
2. Incorrect. Correct version: There was no trouble with the performance; everything went smoothly.
3. Incorrect. Correct version: I didn't go to the movies last night, although I wanted to.
4. Incorrect. Correct version: The show was postponed, due to the lead actor getting sick.
5. Correct. As long as you promise not to tell anybody, I will tell you.
6. Incorrect. Correct version: Waiting for the class to end is boring.
7. Correct. I like playing basketball, but I'm not very good at it.
8. Incorrect. Correct version: I like playing basketball, but I'm not very good at it.
9. Correct. The company launched a new product; it quickly gained popularity in the market.
10. Incorrect. Correct version: The company launched a new product and it quickly gained popularity in the market.

Task 17. Page 38. Are the following sentences correct? If not, write the correct version below.

1. Correct. These animals are all amphibians: frogs, salamanders, newts and toads.
2. Correct. There is only one answer to the: problem sell your house.
3. Incorrect. Correct version: I love France: it's beautiful and it has delicious food.
4. Incorrect. Correct version: At the break of dawn, the majestic mountain range revealed itself in all its splendor: snow-capped peaks glimmering in the golden hues of the rising sun.
5. Incorrect. Correct version: The winners of this week's school quiz are: Jane, Imran and Felix.
6. Incorrect. Correct version: Anderson didn't know whether to order pizza, pasta or fried rice.
7. Incorrect. Correct version: She got what she deserved: a new car and a fancy house.
8. Incorrect. Correct version: Kingsley needs to improve his use of the present perfect.
9. Correct. There were stone pillars standing in the field: the ruins of an ancient castle.

Your turn. Page 40. Example answers.

1. The dog's bone.
2. The boys' changing room.
3. I don't like maths.

Task 18. Page 41. Are the following sentences correct? If not, write the correct version.

1. Incorrect. Correct version: The dog's leash is too long.
2. Incorrect. Correct version: It's a beautiful day outside.
3. Incorrect. Correct version: They're going to the park tomorrow.
4. Incorrect. Correct version: The boys' changing room is out of order.
5. Incorrect. Correct Version: He's the best at what he does.

6. Incorrect. Correct version: Whose book is this?
7. Incorrect. Correct version: We went to John's party last night.
8. Incorrect. Correct version: I'm looking forward to the weekends.
9. Incorrect. Correct version: The swans were flying high over the river.

Task 19. Page 42. The following are situations in which an exclamation mark could be used. Think of a suitable exclamation for each situation.

Example: Lost – "Help! I think I'm lost!"
Finding buried treasure. Hey, look what I've found!
Riding a roller coaster for the first time. Oh, this is amazing!
Receiving a surprise gift. Aww, thanks a million!
Witnessing a meteor shower. Wow! That's incredible.
Solving a difficult puzzle. Yes I've done it!
Discovering a hidden passage. Look! This is fantastic!
Meeting your favourite celebrity. I'm so pleased to meet you!
Winning a lottery jackpot. Hurray!

Task 20. Page 45. Add varied punctuation. Suggested answer.

In the heart of the forest, a symphony of nature's sounds harmonised the sweet song of starlings; the gentle whispers of the wind and the babbling of the brook echoed through the valley. A kaleidoscope of colours stretched out before me: vibrant bluebells carpeted the meadow and a burst of reds, yellows and purples fluttered, as butterflies danced upon the petals. Like a friendly guardian, the sun cast its warm embrace upon the earth, its golden rays gently caressing the treetops creating a shimmering array of light and shadow.... how marvellous! Sandwiched between moss and ivy, a stone path led the way up to a ruined castle – still standing defiantly as a proud testimony to a former age.

Task 21. Page 47. Read the following morning routine of Oscar. Underline all the verbs.

At 6:30 am Oscar's day <u>begins</u> with the sound of his alarm, and he <u>hops</u> out of bed with youthful energy. At 6:45, after a quick shower, he <u>grabs</u> a cereal bar and <u>rushes</u> to get dressed for school. Oscar's school bus <u>arrives</u> at 7:30 and he <u>heads off</u> for a day of learning. At school, Oscar <u>attends</u> classes, <u>participates</u> in football, and <u>socialises</u> with his friends during lunch breaks. At 3:30 pm, once back home, Oscar <u>completes</u> his homework assignments and then <u>goes</u> out to play football.

Now re-write the passage in the past tense, beginning with "Yesterday…". The first sentence has been done for you.

Yesterday Oscar's day began with the sound of his alarm. He hopped out of bed with youthful energy. At 6:45, after a quick shower, he grabbed a cereal bar and rushed to get dressed for school. Oscar's school bus arrived at 7:30 and he headed off for a day of learning. At school, Oscar attended classes, participated in football, and socialised with his friends during lunch breaks. At 3:30 pm, once back home, Oscar completed his homework assignments and then went out to play football.

Re-write the sentences in the past tense. P.48

1. They lived in a big house.
2. He walked to school every day.
3. I ate breakfast at 7 am.
4. The sun rose in the East.
5. We played tennis at weekend.
6. She visited her grandmother.
7. The train departed at 8.30 am.
8. They spoke English fluently.
9. The birds sang in the morning.
10. They dreamed of being rich.
11. He drove to work.
12. I climbed the mountain.
13. The church bells rang.
14. We swam often.
15. She always forgot her way.
16. Tom gave his money away.
17. They tried hard.
18. The birds soared.
19. They were friendly.
20. The day was beautiful.

Task 22. Page 49. This passage has inconsistent tenses. Re-write it putting all the <u>main verbs</u> into the past tense.

Nestled high in the rugged embrace of the mountains, a picturesque scene **<u>unfolded</u>** before my eyes. Towering pine trees, their dark green needles swaying gently in the breeze, **<u>framed</u>** the foreground of this majestic landscape. Vibrant wildflowers **<u>carpeted</u>** the ground, offering a kaleidoscope of colours – tulips, daisies, and heather **<u>danced</u>** in harmony, creating a vibrant scene that **<u>beckoned</u>** me to explore further. At the heart of this wilderness, a pristine alpine lake **<u>glistened</u>** in the midday sun, its waters mirroring the azure sky above. A crystal-clear stream **<u>fed</u>** the lake, its gentle babbling providing a soothing soundtrack to this natural sanctuary. Above, the sun **<u>hung</u>** like a radiant jewel in a flawless sapphire sky, casting a warm, golden glow over the entire scene. As I **<u>looked</u>** up, I **<u>spotted</u>** eagles soaring with effortless grace, their powerful wings painting lazy circles in the endless azure sky above.

Task 23. Page 54. Change "tell" into "show" sentences adding as much detail as possible.

Tell: The temperature fell and it started to snow.
Show: The air chilled, and delicate snowflakes drifted down from the leaden sky, transforming the landscape into a tranquil winter wonderland.

Tell: The garden looked beautiful and smelled so sweet.
Show: Vibrant blossoms adorned the garden, their hues creating a visual symphony, while the air carried the sweet, intoxicating fragrance of blooming flowers.

Tell: The man was old and looked tired.
Show: Wrinkles etched a map of time on the man's face, and weariness lingered in the lines around his eyes. Fatigue painted a silent narrative, casting shadows on his once-vibrant spirit.

Tell: The hurricane had destroyed the town.
Show: Debris scattered like the aftermath of chaos, buildings reduced to skeletal remnants as the hurricane's wrath swept through, leaving behind a town in ruins.

Tell: It was night time. The castle was creepy.
Show: In the cloak of night, the castle emerged, its ominous silhouette adorned with spires that seemed to reach for the darkness. An eerie ambiance whispered through the air, casting an unsettling pallor over the ancient structure.

Tell: The city was very busy with people. There were lots of sounds and smells.
Show: Within the bustling city, a river of humanity flowed through crowded streets, each person contributing to the lively mix of urban life. The air pulsed with a plethora of sounds — a symphony of footsteps, conversations, and distant traffic, as sweet aromas wafted through the air.

Tell: The lake was beautiful.
Show: The lake sprawled beneath the open sky, its surface reflecting a breathtaking panorama of colours. Sunlight danced upon the water, painting a shimmering masterpiece that celebrated the natural beauty of the serene landscape.

Tell: The room was abandoned and filthy.
Show: Dust settled on forgotten surfaces in the empty, forlorn room. The air hung heavy with the musty scent of disuse, and the floor echoed with the hushed whispers of neglect.

Tell: Miriam was sad.
Show: A dark cloud had hung over Miriam all day. She felt as if the weight of the world was on her shoulders. As the day went on, she descended lower and lower. A long frown developed on her usually smiling face. Tears rolled down her cheeks.

Identify sound-related words. Page 59.

An orchestra of worker bees buzzed and hummed their way around the hibiscus and honeysuckle, accompanied by a lively choir of sparrows and starlings above. As the water fountain continued its ceaseless splashing and chattering, a tranquil breeze whispered through the vines: the serenity was disturbed only by the occasional yelps of a nearby dog or the faint whir of a distant jet plane.

The words highlighted in yellow are words which express sounds. Notice that some of the words (highlighted in blue) are not themselves sounds but things which are closely associated with a particular sound by their nature. So, by describing the presence of a water fountain you are also evoking the sound in the reader's mind. In addition, we have not simply mentioned "bees" and "birds" but have been more detailed and specific in our descriptions – "worker bees", "sparrows" and "starlings". This helps the reader to get a more vivid picture.

Brainstorm smell-related words. Page 60.

Perfume, roses, lavender, jasmine, lilac, peony, lily, iris, sweet pea, marigold, herbs, basil, mint, thyme, rosemary, lemon, orange, apples, lime, bergamot, pine, cedar, moss, soil, vanilla, honeysuckle, summer fruits, clove, freshly cut grass, eucalyptus, coffee, tea, barbecue smells, e.g. hot dogs, onions, grilled chicken, sweetcorn.

Brainstorm touch-related words. Page 61.

Bumpy, slippery, fuzzy, craggy, grainy, lumpy, gritty, rocky, bristly, smooth, creamy, bushy, hairy, fluffy, glossy, silky, velvety, slimy, feathery, watery, waxy, thorny, soggy, soft, hard, spikey, soapy, squidgy, serrated, sharp, rough, pebbly, oily, jagged, leathery, lumpy, firm, fury, delicate, coarse, cobbled, crocodilian, crooked, crusty, abrasive, barbed, bristly. Wrinkly, steely.

Task 24. Page 63. Identify one of each of the following language devices in the passage below.

Simile: like drowsy dancers; like a ribbon of dreams.
Hyperbole: millions upon millions; thousand stories.
Alliteration: sun stretched; petals, persuading; drowsy dancers;
Metaphor: moss-carpeted; garden's confetti.
Personification: played its morning chorus; golden arms; persuading; roses dancing with glee; daffodils whispering; wise branches; bees humming in conversation; leaves applauding.
Onomatopoeia buzzed; hummed.
Note: Personification is a form of metaphor so some of the personifications can also be metaphors.

Research the writer's name. Page 64.

"I wandered lonely as a cloud" William Wordsworth.
"Old Marley was as dead as a doornail." Charles Dickens.
"As constant as the northern star." William Shakespeare (Julias Ceasar).

Task 25. Page 65. Think of a suitable word or phrase to complete the similes. Suggested answers.

As tough as an old boot.
As slippery as a sardine.
As fast as a dart.
As sharp as a sword.
As dopey as a sleepy sloth.
As reliable as reinforced steel.
As quiet as a sleeping baby.
As sparkly as a sapphire.
As bright as a carpet of crystals.
As hot as a fireball.
As light as a feather.
As stubborn as tired donkey.
She moved as gracefully as a swan.
His laughter was as melodious as birdsong.

Task 26. Page 66. Complete these similes with a suitable word or phrase.

The moon looked like a hanging pearl.
I rolled out of bed like a reluctant rock.
The lake was like a sparkling mirror.
The house was like a large beast waiting to pounce against the dark horizon.
The sky was like a floating swimming pool.
The clouds were like cotton-candy.
It was so hot it was like living in an oven.
It was so cold it was like living in a fridge.
The night was as black as the abyss where light dare not tread.
Wrinkles covered the man's face like crevasses.
The movie was so boring it was like watching paint dry.
I leapt across the floor like kangaroo on a pogo stick.
I sped off like a bolt of lightening.
His smile lit up the room like a spotlight.

Task 27. Page 68. Read each example below. Choose whether you think it's a simile or a metaphor and then explain what two things are being compared.

1. The sky was like a sapphire quilt.
This is an example of a simile where the sky is compared to a sapphire quilt.

2. Her tears were a river of sorrow.

This is an example of a metaphor where tears are compared to a river.

3. Time is a thief in the night.

This is an example of a metaphor where time is compared to a thief.

4. His anger was like a volcano waiting to erupt.

This is an example of a simile where his anger is compared to a volcano waiting to erupt.

Task 28. Page 69. Below are lots of words and phrases which can be made into metaphors. Use the words to try to produce at least 10 metaphors by mixing and matching.

Metaphor: Hope is a light in the darkness.

1. Her smile was a beacon of light in darkness.
2. Love is a rollercoaster.
3. Jim's stomach is a bottomless pit.
4. Trust is a bridge built over time.
5. The snow-covered field was a carpet of diamonds.
6. Life is a journey.
7. Laughter is music of the soul.
8. Salma has a heart of gold.
9. Time is a river flowing endlessly.
10. Billy is a breath of fresh air.

The Raven. Page 71.

Once upon a midnight dreary, while I pondered, weak and weary,
Over many a quaint and curious volume of forgotten lore—
While I nodded, nearly napping, suddenly there came a tapping,
As of someone gently rapping, rapping at my chamber door.
"'Tis some visitor," I muttered, "tapping at my chamber door—
Only this and nothing more."

Ah, distinctly I remember it was in the bleak December;
And each separate dying ember wrought its ghost upon the floor.
Eagerly I wished the morrow;—vainly I had sought to borrow
From my books surcease of sorrow—sorrow for the lost Lenore—
For the rare and radiant maiden whom the angels name Lenore—
Nameless here for evermore.

And the silken, sad, uncertain rustling of each purple curtain
Thrilled me—filled me with fantastic terrors never felt before;

So that now, to still the beating of my heart, I stood repeating
"'Tis some visitor entreating entrance at my chamber door—
Some late visitor entreating entrance at my chamber door;—
This it is and nothing more."

Presently my soul grew stronger; hesitating then no longer,
"Sir," said I, "or Madam, truly your forgiveness I implore;
But the fact is I was napping, and so gently you came rapping,
And so faintly you came tapping, tapping at my chamber door,
That I scarce was sure I heard you"—here I opened wide the door;—
Darkness there and nothing more.

Task 30. Page 72. Complete these sentences with suitably hyperbolic words or phrases.

1. The building was so big it was practically touching the stars.
2. I was so tired, I slept like a baby.
3. The journey was so long. It seemed to last forever.
4. I'm so busy, I have a million things to do.
5. He's skinnier than a rake.
6. She cried for weeks.
7. I have to go to the shop but I'll be back in 2 seconds.
8. That is the most beautiful dress in the world.
9. You are in England and someone says: "She was screaming so loud, you could hear her in Australia."
10. I was so embarrassed I nearly died.
11. You are the best friend in the universe.
12. That racing car was so fast it was gone in a flash.

Task 31. Page 73. Underline all the examples of onomatopoeia in the sentences below.

The windows rattled in their frames, creating an eerie symphony of sound.

The distant boom of explosions echoed through the valley.

The peace was disturbed by the clattering of cups and plates coming from the kitchen.

The glass shattered when he rested his cup on it.

Sizzling sweetcorn hissed on the crackling campfire as the wind whirred over the trees.

All around, the air was filled with the soft music of buzzing bees and chirping birds.

The thunder rumbled loudly in the distance as the storm approached.

The bees buzzed around the colourful garden, collecting nectar from the flowers.

The baby giggled with delight as the puppy's tail thumped against the floor.

The sizzling bacon in the frying pan made my mouth water.

The old floorboards creaked underfoot as we tiptoed through the haunted house.

Task 32. Page 74. Make your own sentences using onomatopoeia.

1. The old windows began to rattle as the strong wind swept through the house.
2. A distant boom echoed through the valley, signalling the arrival of a summer storm.
3. The clatter of dishes filled the kitchen as the chef prepared a lively meal.
4. The delicate vase slipped from her hands and shattered into fragments.
5. In the kitchen, the bacon started to sizzle and pop on the hot frying pan.
6. As the campfire crackled, sparks danced in the night, creating a mesmerising display.
7. The computer whirred as it processed data.
8. In the serene forest, the trees seemed to whisper secrets to each other in the gentle breeze.
9. The old door creaked as it swung open reluctantly.
10. Among the autumn leaves, the critters moved, creating a soft rustle in the underbrush.

Task 33. Page 78. Re-write the paragraph below using a range of different openers. Aim to include verbs, adjectives, adverbs, prepositions and similes as your openers.

On a journey to a distant place, I set off with nothing but my map and a compass. Meandering through the village, cute cottages and exquisite hedgerows line the way. Like the perfume of paradise, sweet aromas arise from the gardens while music echoes from the sky above where the sparrows hover. Charming lanes take me over a fast-flowing rivers and through deep, grassy valleys. Above, the sun is dripping heat and the sky is smiling. Gently, the wind strokes my face.

Task 34. Page 85. Suggested answer.

In the shrouded embrace of the night, a gothic castle loomed, its spires reaching into the inky darkness like skeletal fingers clawing at the heavens. A veil of mist, as chilling as the breath of an ice-demon, cloaked the ancient fortress, obscuring its sinister secrets. Charcoal clouds clung to the moon, leaving the night in shades of spectral gray, while the salty stench of the nearby ocean hung in the air, intermingling with the damp earth.

Circling above, bat cranked their wings through the mist like malevolent spirits – their screeches echoed eerily through the desolate landscape, interrupting the silence. The rocks beneath, weathered and worn, bore witness to centuries of tumultuous tides, standing as stoic sentinels against the relentless sea.

From the castle's ghost-white windows, a dim glow shone, casting long shadows that danced like ancient ghosts over the rocks; within, a cacophony of howls and screams reverberated, as if the very walls themselves were crying with pain. Through the mist, the silhouette of a figure emerged, cloaked in darkness, like

Task 35. Page 91.

Read the short story in the box below and then see if you can identify the different elements of the plot structure on the next page.

Boastful Brian always thought he was the best at everything. He went around school stating there's no dare he wouldn't do and no challenge he wouldn't take.
One day, his friend Jackson dared him into a challenge. "There's a door at the back of the school hall that says, 'DANGER! DO NOT ENTER'. I dare you to open that door."
At first, Brian didn't want to take the dare, but Jackson wouldn't stop teasing him. Finally, Brian reluctantly agreed to open the door and cautiously moved towards it with outstretched arm.
With a sudden pull, Brian flung open the door and immediately fell back in horror. Scores of poisonous snakes escaped and spread across the school, biting everyone in their path. Brian was bitten and poisoned and had to be rushed off to receive emergency medical care. For a number of hours, his life was in the balance. Fortunately, he received treatment just in time. Brian recovered and travelled home to his family. He slept a long sleep. When he woke, he promised never to take a stupid dare again and to change his boastful ways. He had learned his lesson once and for all.

Plot elements: exposition, inciting incident, rising action, climax, falling action, resolution.

Scores of poisonous snakes escaped and spread across the school, biting everyone in their path. Brian was bitten and poisoned and had to be rushed off to receive emergency medical care. For a number of hours, his life was in the balance.

Climax

Brian recovered and travelled home to his family. He slept a long sleep.

Falling action

When he woke, he promised never to take a stupid dare again and to change his boastful ways. He had learned his lesson once and for all.

Resolution

Finally, Brian reluctantly agreed to open the door and cautiously moved towards it with outstretched arm.

Rising action

Boastful Brian always thought he was the best at everything. He went around school stating there's no dare he wouldn't do and no challenge he wouldn't take.

Exposition

One day, his friend Jackson dared him into a challenge. "There's a door at the back of the school hall that says, 'DANGER! DO NOT ENTER'. I dare you to open that door."

Inciting incident

Task 36. Page 100. Write a setting for a haunted castle.

What time of year is it?

What can you see?

What time of day is it?

What is the weather like?

Any unusual smells?

What might you find here?

Does the castle or location have a name?

What is the atmosphere? How does the place make you feel?

Write a simile about the place.

What can you hear?

Now write up your setting as a paragraph.

____

____

____

____

____

____

Task 37. Page 90. Annotate the passage below which is a description of setting from Dickens' *A Christmas Carol*. Highlight Anything that you think is effective.

Once upon a time—of all the good days in the year, on Christmas Eve—old Scrooge sat busy in his counting-house. It was cold, bleak, biting weather: foggy withal: and he could hear the people in the court outside, go wheezing up and down, beating their hands upon their breasts, and stamping their feet upon the pavement stones to warm them. The city clocks had only just gone three, but it was quite dark already—it had not been light all day—and candles were flaring in the windows of the neighbouring offices, like ruddy smears upon the palpable brown air. The fog came pouring in at every chink and keyhole, and was so dense without, that although the court was of the narrowest, the houses opposite were mere phantoms. To see the dingy cloud come drooping down, obscuring everything, one might have thought that Nature lived hard by, and was brewing on a large scale.

Engaging Introduction: Opening immediately captures reader's attention with the timeless fairy tale beginning of "Once upon a time." The specific mention of Christmas Eve sets the stage for the holiday theme, signalling a significant time for the narrative.

Character Placement: Scrooge in his counting-house establishes main location for the scene, emphasising his preoccupation with business and setting the tone for his character.

Time Reference: Reference to the city clocks emphasises lateness of the hour, creating sense of the approaching night and contributing to the overall mood.

Descriptive Weather: Use of adjectives like "cold," "bleak," "biting" effectively conveys harshness of the weather. The description of fog adds atmosphere creating sense of isolation & chill.

Sensory Details: People wheezing, beating hands, stamping feet brings the scene to life with sensory details. Readers can feel the discomfort and coldness of the environment.

Metaphorical Language: The use of metaphorical language comparing the fog to a "dingy cloud" coming down like a curtain enhances the vividness of the description. The metaphor of Nature "brewing on a large scale" adds a whimsical touch, blending natural and supernatural elements.

Contrast of Darkness: Contrast between darkness outside and candles flaring in the windows adds visual interest. Imagery of "ruddy smears upon palpable brown air" conveys warmth in contrast to the cold & dark surroundings.

Task 38. Page 106. Read this description of Ebeneezer Scrooge from Charles Dickens' novella A Christmas Carol. Go through it carefully and annotate it with the help of the boxes.

"Oh! But he was a tight-fisted hand at the grindstone, Scrooge! a squeezing, wrenching, grasping, scraping, clutching, covetous, old sinner! Hard and sharp as flint, from which no steel had ever struck out generous fire; secret, and self-contained, and solitary as an oyster. The cold within him froze his old features, nipped his pointed nose, shrivelled his cheek, stiffened his gait; made his eyes red, his thin lips blue; and spoke out shrewdly in his grating voice. A frosty rime was on his head, and on his eyebrows, and his wiry chin. He carried his own low temperature always about with him; he iced his office in the dog-days; and didn't thaw it one degree at Christmas."

Symbolism: The description is rich in symbolism, portraying Scrooge as a cold, frozen figure. The imagery of the frosty rime on his head, eyebrows, and wiry chin reinforces his icy nature and lack of warmth.

Vivid imagery: Dickens uses vivid images to describe Scrooge; "tight-fisted hand at the grindstone," "squeezing, wrenching, grasping," and "clutching, covetous, old sinner" convey the miserly and greedy nature of Scrooge.

Figurative language (metaphors / similes): Use of devices, such as "hard and sharp as flint," or "solitary as an oyster", creates strong visual and tactile impression. This extends to describe his features, nose, cheek, gait, eyes, and lips, enhancing overall characterisation.

Alliteration & repetition: Dickens uses alliteration & repetition to emphasise Scrooge's negative qualities. Repetition of harsh consonant sounds in "squeezing," "wrenching," "grasping," and alliterative "secret", "self-contained" and "solitary" adds a rhythmic quality, making it more impactful.

Character traits: Description gives a big list of Scrooge's characteristics, including being secret, self-contained, solitary, and covetous. These traits contribute to a detailed and vivid portrayal of the character, allowing readers to relate more easily to him.

Physical effects of his personality:
Dickens links Scrooge's personality to physical effects on his appearance. The coldness within him is said to freeze his features, nip his nose, shrivel his cheek, and stiffen his gait. Links his inner nature and external appearance adding depth to the character.

Thank you for your support.

© 2024. Dr Phil's English. All rights reserved.
Purchase of this resource entitles the purchaser to reproduce the pages in limited quantities for single classroom use only. Duplication for an entire school or for commercial purposes is strictly forbidden without written permission from the publisher. Copying any part of this product and placing it on the internet in any form (even a personal / classroom website) is strictly forbidden and is a violation of the Digital Millennium Copyright Act (DMCA) (United States) or the Copyright, Designs & Patents Act 1988 (United Kingdom).
You may:
Use this item for personal / student use in a single classroom.
Purchase licenses at a big discount for others to use this resource.
Enjoy this product for years to come.
You may not:
Give this item to your friends or colleagues
Copy this item for use by others.
Post this item on a website for download. This includes personal websites, district websites, Amazon Inspire, etc.
Post this item or any life copy for sale or for free.